THE RECOVERY OF MAN IN CHILDHOOD

THE RECOVERY OF MAN IN CHILDHOOD

A Study in the Educational Work of Rudolf Steiner

A. C. HARWOOD

When I was a child, I spake as a child,
I felt as a child, I thought as a child.

LONDON
HODDER & STOUGHTON

Made and Printed in Great Britain
for Hodder & Stoughton Ltd
by Jarrold and Sons Ltd, Norwich

TO MY VERY GOOD FRIEND

H.A.W.M.

Contents

Advice on Terminology

A LARGE part of this book refers directly to the organisation of the Schools called indifferently Waldorf Schools from the first one founded in Stuttgart, or Rudolf Steiner Schools from the name of their originator.

It is characteristic of these schools to cover the whole of childhood. The Nursery Class is from the age of about four to six. Children commonly enter the Main School between six and seven and continue with the same teacher through eight Classes or Grades up to the age of fourteen. After this come four Grades in the Upper School or High School, terminating with the twelfth, equivalent to the Sixth Form of English tradition.

The American terms *Grade* and *High School* have been used equally with the English *Class* and *Upper School.* I have also used the convenient and pleasant American word *sibling* for a younger brother or sister.

A.C.H.

I acknowledge with gratitude my indebtedness to the Myrin Institute of New York which made the writing of this book possible.

CHAPTER I

Premises

So many books on Education have been written in modern times that anyone who ventures to add another volume to this vast library must have valid reasons for his temerity. The justification for the present work is that it is an attempt to present a comprehensive account of what lies behind an educational movement of growing importance and authority. It is the movement deriving from the work of the Austrian philosopher, scientist and seer, Rudolf Steiner, whose life spanned the second half of the last century and the first quarter of this, and whose genius, though steeped in the knowledge of his age, so far transcended it that his own generation found it difficult to give him recognition. For it was his fate, and his distinction, to be a scientist among artists and an artist among scientists, a universal genius in an age of specialists, a spiritual investigator among the still triumphant explorers of the physical world. Not many people even know that Steiner's work in the educational field has led to the foundation of schools in all parts of the world;[1] and, even where this is known, there is scant understanding for the conception of man and child on which they are based.

Yet no-one can appreciate what is being attempted in these schools unless he takes the trouble (it is an exhilarating and rewarding trouble) to investigate some of the central formative ideas in Steiner's philosophy. For there never was an educational movement in which practice more closely embodies theory, in which the smallest part more accurately reflects the organic whole. Yet Steiner's philosophy was not itself developed in the educational field. It grew during a varied life, in which he was now engaged in the Goethe Archives in Weimar, now lecturing to a Working Men's College in Berlin, now editing a leading literary periodical, now forming his own society and designing a unique building, perhaps the most original of the modern age, for its headquarters. It was only at the conclusion of the First World War, in response to the request of a leading German industrialist,

[1] At the time of writing about 60 schools educating some 30,000 children.

that Steiner entered the sphere of children's education by inaugurating the Waldorf School in Stuttgart, intended primarily for the children of the workers in a cigarette factory. Nor was this direct entry of a philosophy into practice confined to education. At about the same time agriculturalists, doctors, actors and members of other professions were approaching Steiner for new impulses in their respective branches of life. Parallel accounts could be written of development in all these fields.

It is not easy for the modern mind to understand how a single man could enter effectively into such varied activities. In Platonic language it would have been said that Steiner was the philosopher who ascended into the realm of Ideas, where the ultimate unity of all things is to be found. It could equally be expressed by saying that he approached all fields of experience with new forms of perception and new modes of thinking. In studying Steiner we have constantly to remind ourselves that our own forms of perception and modes of thought have only come into being in the last few centuries, that the world looked and felt quite different to our not very remote forefathers, who saw sun, moon and planets as boundary signs of spheres enveloping a central earth, who spoke of the 'virtues' of plants and the 'affinities' of substances, who had no mathematical interpretation of matter and its forces. It is not a question of our own age being 'right' and former ages 'wrong'; but our form of consciousness embraces other things and sees in other modes than that of former times. It is when we make ourselves aware of earlier changes in human consciousness that we also make ourselves sensitive to new forms of thought and perception which may emerge, and indeed are emerging, from our present interpretation of man and nature.

It is with such emergent modes of thinking and perception that Steiner was concerned. There is therefore a double task awaiting anyone who endeavours to interpret his thought to a new public. He has not only to mediate new thoughts to his readers but in order to do so he has, in some sense, to initiate them into new ways of thinking. In this process one of the first things which the reader will discover is that he is being asked to think artistically and imaginatively not only about poetry or painting but also about the Sciences, that the principle of form is regarded as the creative and controlling power in works of nature as well as in works of art, that a new science is being based on qualitative aspects of the material world no less than the present science is based on the quantitative.

In its very nature, therefore, Steiner's educational philosophy stands in the centre of one of the great questions of modern education, the mutual relation of the Sciences and the Arts. It is certainly to be deplored that many people's outlook on life is almost entirely based on the Sciences, while that of others is equally limited to the Arts or Humanities. It is no solution, however, to ask that everyone shall be equally educated in both, as they are at present understood. The tension between the two worlds shifts its ground but remains unresolved. It can only be properly released when a disciplined artistic perception becomes part of the method of natural science, and when the healthy objectivity of the Sciences penetrates those finer feelings on which the life of the Humanities finally rests. Such a marriage of the Arts and Sciences, a marriage in the core of their being, based on the ultimate unity of human experience, is one of the great essential themes of a Steiner education.

It is to be found, for instance, in the way in which Steiner has developed in all spheres of life the principle of metamorphosis which he first studied when he was called upon to edit the scientific works of Goethe, the last genius who was Master alike in the Sciences and the Arts. Indeed Steiner's account of childhood itself is instinct with this very principle. He did not believe that the faculties of a child's mind develop from like beginnings, but that in the alchemy of growth one quality is changed into another, in the same way as Goethe spoke of the metamorphosis of the green leaf into the coloured petal of the flower.

To give more examples than this single one of Steiner's mode of thinking in an introductory chapter would be to anticipate the argument of the book. Even to mention this single principle of metamorphosis is to fall into the danger which Steiner himself always strove sedulously to avoid—the danger of abstraction. For it must be added in conclusion that Steiner's ideas about childhood (and about other things as well) are not theories or hypotheses in the ordinary sense of modern science. They came to him with the force of immediate and overwhelming experience. There is a vast difference between observing a process from outside and realising it through conscious participation. Modern child psychologists take the former path. They have invented a host of techniques and constructed the most ingenious apparatus for examining children from without. But everyone has some conscious memories of childhood and carries within him unconsciously the results of his childhood experiences. It would never occur to a modern educator to strengthen by exercise and meditation the inner power of memory so that the forgotten experiences and unconscious forces of childhood became conscious experience to him. This, however (together with much else of the same character), is the kind of thing which Steiner claims to have done, so that what he says about childhood is born of immediate perception and not of intellectual theory.

To enter into the experience of others requires not only understanding but imaginative sympathy as well. Logical thoughts can pass immediately from mind to mind. To communicate experience is a matter of art, which has indeed its own logic but which never speaks from mind to mind without evoking deeper qualities of feeling. Anyone who attempts this task in the sphere of education must feel, like the bards of old, the need of an inspiring genius, and, if he is essaying nothing less than a complete saga of childhood, will wish, like Homer, to preface his book with the devout invocation: *Sing, Muse, the Child.*

CHAPTER II

Growth and Consciousness

THERE are a great many ways of looking at the complex processes of childhood, and it is only possible in a single book to deal with some of them, and then only one at a time. We will begin with the most obvious, the question of the growth of mind and body.

In ordinary educational theory these are regarded as fundamentally continuous and parallel, although psychologists do note periods of what seems like a setback in general development. Much psychological experiment is devoted to finding out the age at which adult mental faculties appear in the child, as well as to the question of whether a child learns through experience or by simple 'maturation'. Children artificially retarded in some activity, such as a special use of the limbs, show an outstanding ability to catch up with other children when the restraint is removed—as indeed anyone would expect, provided the experiment is not carried too far. It is not only unpardonable but also unnecessary to make such experiments, when historical cases can be found of children who have been subjected to precocious development or exceptional retardation.

In general, however, the educator today takes the different manifestations of the psyche to be found in adult life—thought, memory, emotions, etc.—and looks for their emergence in the life of children. One of the good results of such observations is that we discover how slowly they do arise. Take, for instance, the simplest form of abstract thinking in connection with simple numbers. The French psychologist Piaget made experiments to find out how soon children could equate simple numbers represented by such articles as bottles and glasses, or eggs and egg-cups. He found that very few children between the ages of four and six were able to match six bottles with six glasses or six egg-cups with six eggs. When they had been helped to do so, or when, in a few cases, they had been able to match the articles correctly, a still stranger event occurred. If the bottles were placed closer together and the glasses spaced more widely and the children were asked if there were still the same number of each, they almost invariably replied that there were now more glasses. If the process were reversed, they said there were more bottles! It was generally only after the age of six that the children were able to see that the number of bottles and glasses remained constant.

It is not good to make even these simple experiments with children, because it lies in the nature of the case that you must expect them to do something unnatural to their age for which their minds are not yet ripe. It is as though you asked them to lift heavy weights before their muscles and sinews were strong enough. But it is a typical example of the way in which experimental psychology tries to observe the emergence of adult faculties in the child.

It is possible, however, to consider the matter from the opposite point of view. Childhood is a time of losing capacities as well as of acquiring them. Growing up is loss as well as gain. Is there some connection between the loss of a childish faculty and the acquisition of an adult one? Perhaps the examination of the process of loss will lead us to a better understanding of childhood than if we approach the child from what is fundamentally an adult standpoint. Let us take only one of these capacities—the small child's gift for imitation.[1] Everyone knows how quickly and eagerly children copy the activities of the life around them. A child must not merely be doing the same *kind* of thing as the adult but it has to be identical. If you are hammering, your small boy must be hammering too. If you put down the hammer and take up a saw, he must have a saw as well. Indeed, the bulk of small children's lives is a copying of the world around them:

> as if their whole vocation
> were endless imitation.

An adult can copy, also, but unless he is a 'born mimic'—an excellent phrase which reveals the origin of imitation—he will make poor work of it compared with the child. The important thing, however, is that when an adult imitates he does it in a different way from the child; he carefully observes and studies the thing he wishes to imitate and does it consciously. The child does no such thing; he imitates instinctively. It might well be thought

[1] It is incredible that some psychologists have denied that children imitate on the grounds that their movements are purely functional and organically determined. What of the child who throws the stub of his chocolate cigarette on the fire?

from their imitative forces that children's sense-perceptions were remarkably acute, but we know that this is not so. Small children will often simply not hear a loud noise which startles the adult; and what difficulty a child has in seeing the thimble perched so obviously on the arm of the easy-chair The flimsiest disguise, such as a cotton-wool beard for Santa Claus, makes it impossible for him to recognise his own father. It is evident that the imitative power of children is not based on acute sense-perception.

Let us consider this power of imitation in one of its greatest and most wonderful aspects, the child's imitation of speech. There is undoubtedly more than imitation at work when a child learns to speak, but nobody can deny that imitation plays a major part. A child learns the speech of the adults around him. Deaf children do not naturally learn to speak at all. If, however, the child's imitation were mere reproduction, a looking-glass image of what he perceives, he would learn to talk like a parrot, but he would not learn to speak. In fact, the small child enters so deeply into the essential nature of speech that by the age of three or four he is using highly complicated inflections and word combinations to express every kind of relationship of space and time. It is hard for children of adolescent age, painfully learning their Latin grammar, to realise that little Roman children of three and four knew their declensions and conjugations and irregular verbs without troubling their heads about the matter at all. There are few things more miraculous than the birth of language in the child.

It is plain that intelligence is here working in an impersonal, effortless way unknown to the adult. How can we picture its operation? The process by which a child learns through imitation —absorption of his surroundings without conscious study or reflection—is the precise opposite to the way in which an adult learns. We are justified then, at any rate as a preliminary hypothesis, in forming a picture of his spiritual organisation equally opposite to the organisation of the adult. The adult is an individual, an ego, experiencing his individuality within the four walls of his physical body, looking out on the world through the doors and windows of the senses and using the brain to reflect on what they tell him. The child is not a self-conscious individual, his consciousness extends beyond the sphere of his little body, he actually lives *into* his immediate surroundings in a way incomprehensible to the adult; his life of thought and feeling is not personal, but is intimately bound up with the life, speech and actions of those who surround him. Hence he learns immediately, not through an intermediary, conscious process. In an impersonal dream-like, or rather sleep-like, way his powers of consciousness are living in his environment. This impersonal consciousness (it would be called the unconscious by modern psychologists) is far abler and wiser than a personal consciousness. It is not a primitive or puny intelligence but a subtle and masterly one which teaches a child so intricate a thing as the use of language.

Modern consciousness has divided the world for each of us into the 'I' and the 'not-I'. We have no understanding of history or of childhood if we think that this division was valid in former ages. The child lives by that kind of immediate participation in his surroundings which some anthropologists[2] are rightly opining to have been the consciousness of early man. Once we understand this we have to revise our opinion both of the child's mind and of his social behaviour. Seen from the adult point of view, the small child is amoral and unsocial. He does not play with other children, he takes away the other child's toy if he is strong enough to do so, he talks in a monologue even when he is side by side with others. But seen from the child's point of view, it is the adult who is unsocial, with his own private and secretive life of thought and feeling, and his inability to enter selflessly into the movements and the forms of speech of the people around him.

The ability of the small child to live impersonally in his surroundings is the obverse of his inability to think personally like the adult. For the whole body of the child is possessed by organic forces of growth, and *personal consciousness and organic activity are the direct antithesis of each other*. It is the brain and nervous system, where organic processes are at their minimum, which are the seat of our modern adult consciousness. We are not conscious in the respiratory organs or the digestive system, which have the task of building up and maintaining the living organic processes in the body. Consciousness only appears in these organs in the form of pain when they are disordered or diseased. Too much consciousness stunts the forces of growth: too much growth dwarfs the powers of consciousness. The little tailor in the fairy-tale is clever: the giant is stupid. It is through intelligence that David overcomes Goliath.

[2] e.g., Levy-Bruhl.

The child cannot enjoy the personal intelligence of the adult because his brain is still plastic and growing. The adult cannot enjoy the child's participation in his surroundings because his personal intelligence thrusts the world from him as an object for contemplation and speculation.

The corollary to the child's immersion in his surroundings is that the influence of his surroundings penetrates him to an equal depth. The personal consciousness of the adult is a defence against his surroundings. He may be irritated or annoyed to exasperation by some continuous noise: but his consciousness keeps it from penetrating into those unconscious spheres where organic processes are taking place within him. The child may appear not even to hear the noise, but it enters so deeply within him that the forces of growth are affected, and perhaps weakened or impaired.

How deep the forces of imitation will go is to be seen in the fact that adopted children often grow up with an astonishing resemblance to one or other—or both—of their foster-parents, while children brought up by foreign servants in a foreign land could often be credited with some native blood. Much that is attributed to heredity is probably due to the unconscious powers of imitation, working even on the physical body.

The same depth of experience in a slightly more conscious form is to be seen in the matter of the child's food. As adults we are conscious only in the first part of digestion, in the mouth. The baby tastes his milk right down to his fingers and toes, as he shows by his ecstatic kickings and stretchings. When a small child places his hand on the top of his head and says, 'I'm full up to here', he really feels the good food permeating his entire body.

It is not only physical sensations which enter deeply into the child's bodily life. Happily, after an era of somewhat arid scientific hygiene, the importance of the mother's life for the very health of the child is being increasingly recognised. The mere presence of the mother is a balm to the child. If she has to leave him in order to go on a necessary journey, he may, and probably will, show no outward sign of grief. A piece of candy at the moment of parting will assuage all his grief, and the kind relation left in charge will write to the mother that Johnny has not once asked after her. But the observant eye will perhaps notice after a few days that he is not quite so blooming. It may even be that after a week or more he will be a little ill. The adult feels the absence of the loved one in his soul, the child in his body.[3]

It follows that all that is living and human and personally related to the child is the best environment for him in his earliest years. The intrusion into the home of the mechanical impersonal voice of radio and gramophone, and of the unreal pictures of television, with their distortion of size and illusion of movement, can only be deplored as far as the small child is concerned. But such considerations belong to a later chapter which will deal with the earlier years of life in greater detail, when the whole picture of childhood has more clearly emerged.

In general we have to recognise in small children a state of body and mind entirely different from the adult's. In the child a preponderance of growth forces and an impersonal participatory consciousness: in the adult the suppression of growth forces and a personal subjective consciousness which sees the world as object. The stages by which the first becomes the second are the first subject of our study.

[3] The principal of a crèche for the children of war-workers in a big industrial town during the Second World War told the author that several children had sickened and died without apparent cause and she attributed their deaths entirely to the absence of the mothers at work in a factory.

CHAPTER III

The Threefold Relation of Body and Mind

It is not sufficient to speak in generalities about the antithesis of physical growth and personal consciousness, or the distinction between the adult's personal and the child's impersonal consciousness. We must endeavour to come to a clear idea of the inter-relation of physical forces and consciousness at different stages of childhood, and of the way in which the impersonal is metamorphosed into the personal consciousness.

A process of growth, however, can only be understood in relation to its final maturity. What is the relation of the grown body to the developed consciousness of the adult? Much of our view of childhood will depend on how we answer this question. It must be answered before we can revert to the changing relationship of growth and consciousness in the child.

It is only in recent centuries that consciousness has been attributed exclusively to the brain and nervous system. It was Descartes who first proclaimed this theory in the seventeenth century—the century in which the modern scientific outlook was really born. We should remember, however, that it was not held in antiquity, nor is it believed by many people today. When the psychologist Jung was staying with the Pueblo Indians, they informed him that the Americans were mad. The reason the Indians gave for this contention is hardly one that we should imagine. It was that 'the Americans believe they think with their brains, but we know that men think with their hearts'.

The invention of telegraph and telephone developed the theory of Descartes in a way of which he never dreamed. For the brain was further equipped with a telegraph system, receiving information by stimulus along the sensory nerves and then sending out its response along the so-called motor nerves. This picture of the operation of the human mind was always strenuously combated by Rudolph Steiner and is now being questioned by leading neurologists.[1] It matters little that, with the fashion of the age, the brain is now depicted as a scanning mechanism rather than a telephone exchange. The average man is so far convinced that consciousness is the concern of the brain alone that he only thinks it ridiculous when he hears that ancient civilisations considered the seat of consciousness to be the liver or the heart.

For these latter organs are believed to have a purely organic function, which is often represented as merely mechanical. Even school-children are shown 'the works' of a man, in which the heart is represented by a pump, the lungs by bellows and the digestion by a furnace. Gesell writes of fathers in general that 'they would like to know what makes a child tick. It degrades neither child nor father to bring mechanical concepts to bear upon the manifold wonders of the child's behaviour.'

The question is not one of degradation, however, but of fact. It can only be right to think of the body as a mechanism if the body is, in fact, mechanical. The first great distinction between a mechanism and an organism is that the latter is capable of growth and of the repair of its form and substance when damaged—a distinction too obvious to be laboured. But the far more important distinction is something which as yet only Rudolf Steiner has fully recognised, namely, that *the whole human body, and not the brain alone, is a vehicle of consciousness.* No mechanism is conscious. Even the electronic brain—the mere name of which shows a dreadful confusion of thought—is no more conscious than a clock or a mouse-trap. It is only a good deal more elaborate. It will only deserve to be called a brain when it can put a problem to the mathematician as well as answering those he puts to it—and which he has conditioned it to answer.

Picturing the body as a mechanism with consciousness confined to the brain—as it is today only too easy to do—has helped to blind people to their own experience. For if any ordinary person would forget popular theory and attend to what he himself experiences, he would have to admit that he feels a strong connection between certain aspects of consciousness and parts of the

[1] At the Meeting of the British Association for the Advancement of Science (1954), Professor Liddell of Oxford stated that 'the movements excited by cortical stimulation can in no sense be equated with the voluntary movements of the intact organism'. See report in *Nature*, Vol. 174, No. 4433, 16th October, 1954.

body other than the brain. In moments of sudden and deep feeling, sorrow or joy, surprise or fear, the quickening of the beat of the heart and the catch of the breath are apparent to everyone. Similarly, a moment of strong resolution demands a firm movement of the limbs, while sudden fear brings a weakness in the pit of the stomach or even an actual movement of the bowels. Naturally, the consciousness which we experience in the heart or the metabolism or the 'reins'—to use a Biblical expression—is different in quality and intensity from that which we experience through the head. It is just that difference which is explained in Steiner's account of what he has called the 'Threefold Man'.

Modern psychologists have divided the operations of Mind into the three somewhat rough and ready spheres of the Conscious, the Subconscious and the Unconscious. They have done an immense service in drawing attention to the fact that what a man consciously experiences is only a fraction of those powers of mind which form his judgments and guide his conduct. Steiner was entirely at one with the psychologists in this conception. His approach to the more hidden aspects of consciousness, however, is somewhat different from theirs. He does not greatly use the terms subconscious and unconscious—names which, after all, are purely negative in their origin and tell us merely what or where a thing is not. He refers us in the first place to three states of consciousness with which we are all familiar: sleeping, dreaming and waking. For even in sleeping there is a slight measure of consciousness without which the thread of memory would snap, and we should awake every day to a new world. In these three we have a polarity between the *almost* complete darkness of sleeping consciousness and the bright light of waking experience, with the dream life as an intermediate term. Dreams may indeed be very vivid, but we do not grasp in dreaming the meaning of the pictures they place before us or why one picture melts into another in endless succession.

There is another sphere in which we have a similar polarity of light and darkness in consciousness with an intermediate term. It is only in thinking that we experience the full light of consciousness. It was in thinking that Descartes, at the dawn of the modern age, found the certainty of his existence—*cogito ergo sum*. Other philosophers would rather place their reliance on a faculty which is as much the opposite of thinking as sleep is of waking—the faculty of the will. For the will is as much distinguished by unconsciousness as thinking is distinguished by consciousness. In willing we may be conscious of our intentions, and of what we have achieved, but the actual process eludes us. We do not even know how the will takes hold of the muscles in order to move an arm. So dark and hidden is the life of the will that some psychologists have even denied its existence. But this is like denying the existence of darkness because it cannot be seen.

There is a third faculty, however, which lies between the bright light of thinking and the darkness of willing—the faculty of feeling. It is often said to be unfortunate that the word feeling has so many meanings. It may equally stand for a sensation, an emotion, or an intuition. But this is only natural when we consider that through its intermediate position feeling penetrates both upwards into consciousness and downwards into the unconscious. Feeling may be described both as the unconscious seeking the light of the conscious and the conscious seeking the universality of the unconscious. It stands between the conscious and the unconscious as the dream stands between waking and sleeping. Whatever the source of the feeling—and like a dream, it may come from a simple sensation or from a lofty psychic experience—we cannot describe it abstractly, but we are impelled to clothe it in pictures.

It is chiefly to the interpretation of these pictures, whether rising from dreams or from the half-conscious life of feeling, that modern analytical psychology has devoted itself. We may note here the difference in technique between this psychology and Steiner's method of spiritual development. The former brings the hidden pictures up into the realm of normal consciousness: the latter takes consciousness into the hidden realm of the pictures. Steiner's disinclination to use the terms unconscious and subconscious is no doubt partly due to the fact that for him these realms became conscious.

Because it is only half revealed to consciousness, it is hard for us to know a feeling clearly ourselves. As feeling holds the balance between thinking and willing it plays a major part in the forming of judgments: but, however consciously we weigh the pros and cons, it is not easy for us to know what finally decides us on a given course of action. It is equally hard for us to communicate the content as apart from the *fact* of our feelings to others, as we so readily communicate the content of a thought.

Sleeping, dreaming and waking, then, are not only a trinity of three states of consciousness which we experience in succession but they live in us contemporaneously. As we go about our daily lives part of us only is awake; another part is dreaming, and a third is asleep. Happily, it is not only the conscious part which guides our steps. Many people have had the experience that some hidden impulse of the will has suddenly taken hold of them and guided them without their conscious participation, sometimes leading them out of some unforeseen danger, sometimes establishing a connection with someone who proves of immense importance in their lives. We may be thankful that we are not dependent alone on the conscious forces of our personal thinking to guide our lives, but that deeper impulses play in from the sleeping sphere of the will.

There is a further trinity which is related to the trinity of thought, feeling and will as these are related to waking, sleeping and dreaming. It is a trinity which appears in the organisation of the human body. It is not easy for the modern mind to grasp this bodily trinity because it calls for a way of thinking somewhat unfamiliar, although it is appearing here and there in modern thought like new growth among the old stubble. The Gestalt theory of psychology which deals with the totality of human behaviour has something of it. The modern zoological view that an animal is not the creature we see at a given moment but *is* all that it does in its life-cycle is a further example of it. It is the faculty of seeing the visible as the expression, or the partial expression, of a greater invisible reality.

In this sense Steiner regarded the brain and the nervous system as the vehicle, not the cause, of the fully wakened consciousness of thinking. Thought is a non-corporeal or spiritual activity, but it requires a physical organ if it is to express itself in a being that has physical existence. Brain and nerve, in whose substance a continual process of decay occurs, create the possibility of awakened consciousness between birth and death.

Where in the human body do we find the organs which are the polar opposite of brain and nerve? First of all in the organs of digestion and metabolism, where the unconscious process of building up new substance is always taking place. We are accustomed to speaking of all these organs as forming together a *digestive system*. It is this digestive (or metabolic) system, so antithetical in its nature to the brain and nervous system, which Steiner regards in the first place as the expression or physical vehicle of the unconscious faculty of will. But in the physical structure of man there is also another antithesis to the brain and nervous system, the organs of free movement—arms, legs and even the lower jaw. Steiner considered these organs as also forming a 'system' no less than the nerves and digestive organs, even though the functional connection between them is not so immediately apparent. He therefore often linked this limb system to the metabolic system as expressing and sustaining the faculty of will. No doubt the relation of will to this system is more difficult to perceive than that of thinking to the brain and nerves. In the last resort it must be experienced if it is to be thoroughly grasped. For the connection is not a close and localised one, like that between the brain and thought, where definite centres can be allocated to particular spheres of consciousness. It is precisely because the will does *not* fully penetrate and inform the physical body that it is so little conscious. Indeed, it reveals itself more in the function of the organ than in the organ itself. It is *how* a man moves his limbs which gives the observer an insight into his character, not so much the limbs themselves. It is the will to live that keeps the organs of life functioning in spite of illness or the most appalling outer conditions.

In the course of this book much will be said of this hidden relation of the will to limb movement and metabolism. The conception is admittedly difficult for a modern mind to grasp in the first instance, as difficult as for the Pueblo Indians to grasp that thinking has anything to do with the brain. Perhaps the Indian and the modern intellectual mind can best meet together in the intermediate sphere, the sphere of feeling.

For feeling also has its physical basis in the human body. Between the head and the digestive organs lie the lungs and the heart, the centres of respiration and blood circulation. That there is a close connection between these latter organs is shown above all in the fact that the functioning of both is rhythmical. There is a natural harmonious interplay between the rhythms of heart and lung. When this is disturbed by violent exercise, there is a period of much discomfort until a new adjustment is made, in what is termed 'second wind'. The rhythm which has its centre in heart and lungs spreads itself throughout the entire body, to the pulse in fingers and toes, as well as to the minute rise and fall—like a miniature tide—in the cerebro-spinal fluid with every breath that we take. It is these rhythmical processes taken in their totality which Steiner has called the *rhythmic system* and to which he refers the life of feeling.

It is easier to experience the connection between the rhythmical system and feeling than that between the limb system and will. For instance, we know that only sudden emotion—such as fear or joy—violently affects the pulse and breath. When we are relieved from some fear it is literally and not only metaphorically true to say 'we breathe again'. All works of art are penetrated with rhythm because it is in artistic creation that feeling reaches its quintessence.

It was thus that Steiner conceived three great interpenetrating systems in the human body which for brevity may be called the head, the rhythmical and the limb systems, and these three (in their several modes) as the bearers and sustainers of the faculties of thought, feeling and will. The head system is the polar opposite of the limb system, as thought is the polar opposite of will. The rhythmical system forms the intermediary term between limb and head, as does feeling between thought and will. It was characteristic of Steiner's thoroughness that he studied the physiology and psychology of these three systems for more than a dozen years before he spoke of them in public. But once he had publicised the conception, he extended the threefold idea to almost every branch of life.

It is of some interest that the poet-philosopher Samuel Taylor Coleridge, who made so many brilliant conjectures, gave a brief exposition of the three systems in his *Aids to Reflection*. 'The cerebral system of the nerves', he writes, 'has its correspondent antithesis in the abdominal system, but hence arises a synthesis of the two in the pectoral system as the intermediary, and, like a drawbridge, at once conductor and boundary.' The cerebral system is the 'seat of cognition': in the pectoral system arise 'emotions, affections and passions': and, of course (though Coleridge is not explicit on this point), the abdominal system supports the life of will.

From whatever aspect one considers these three systems it is remarkable to observe how exactly the rhythmic system mediates between the other two. Consider, for instance, their relation to movement. The head and brain are protected to the highest degree from the shock of moving. When we walk, the elasticity of a whole series of joints prevents the movement from affecting our head. Within the head the brain swims in the cerebro-spinal fluid, and like its travesty, the electronic brain, it has no moving parts. Stillness and rest characterise the head and brain. The limbs, on the other hand, live in free voluntary movement. We may exercise our limbs (as also our metabolism) a great deal one day and not at all the next.

But between the immobile head and the mobile limbs is the sphere where movement never ceases because, being rhythmical, it has also the quality of rest. For rhythm is both rest in movement and movement in rest. It is the rhythmical muscles which never rest and never tire, the muscles which work in heart and lung from our first breath to our last. The more rhythmical we make our movements the less tiring they are. Modern industrial psychologists, who endeavour to make factory work rhythmical, are only copying our ancestors who, with more artistic sensibility, discovered the practical virtues of the sea-shanty, the milking song, and all the innumerable airs which until modern times accompanied every trade and occupation.

Verse sweetens toil, however rude the sound,
All at her work the village maiden sings,
Nor, as she turns the giddy wheel around,
Revolves the sad vicissitude of things.[2]

The same intermediary position of the rhythmical system can be seen in the bones of the chest, which enclose its central organs. The skull is spherical in its tendency, especially the upper part which encloses the brain. The bones of the limbs are radial and reach out into the forces of space from which the skull protects the brain. The ribs, which encase the heart and lungs, are neither spherical nor radial. As they approach the head in their rhythmic sequence they form a more and more complete circle. As they descend towards the limbs the circular form withdraws and loses itself in the line of the lowest vertebrae.

Psychologically, it is remarkable how exactly the life of feeling,

[2] Richard Gyford *apud* Boswell.

intermediate between thought and will, exemplifies the description by Coleridge of the pectoral system as 'at once a conductor and a boundary'—the drawbridge which may either provide easy access or prove an impassable obstacle. When we love someone, or have enthusiasm for a cause, how easily the thought passes into action. Conversely, when we feel distaste or repugnance, how quickly obstacles arise, how prone we are to forget the unpleasant duty or to find excellent reasons for putting off the unrelished interview. In introducing a new subject to children the greatest pains should be taken to awaken and sustain that interest and enthusiasm which they are always prepared to give to anything new. It may well depend on this whether their feeling life becomes bridge or barrier to some field of knowledge for the whole of their lives.

We have seen that the dreaming nature of feeling and the sleeping nature of will are due to the fact that they are less intensely and locally related to the physical body. But this very fact gives them unique possibilities. They may bring us into relation with worlds outside us not accessible to the self-supporting activity of thinking. Inspirations and intuitions, coming from where we know not, flow into our life of feeling and will, bringing us wisdom in judgment and action far beyond anything we could achieve in personal intellectual thought. It may happen that inspiration or intuition penetrate into the realm of thought and light up in our consciousness as idea. This does not necessarily mean, however, that their source is in the realm of thinking. For above all we must never imagine that the powers of thought, feeling and will can ever live in isolation from each other. There is no thought which is not penetrated by a measure of feeling and will, however attenuated; no will devoid of a trace of thought and feeling; no feeling which does not in some subtle sense play upwards into our thinking consciousness and downwards into the will. Moreover, there is the same absolute interpenetration in the threefold system of the body. Through the nerves a measure of consciousness is present everywhere in the body; the blood brings an element of will even into the finer organs of sense; rhythmical processes penetrate even into the brain. There would be no unity of experience if the interpenetration of spiritual powers and their correspondent physical systems were not complete both within themselves and between each other.

It is only in the adult that all three systems of the threefold organism have reached their maturity. One of the great differences between the child and the grown-up is in the child's different relationship to his threefold nature. We must now consider this difference in connection with the child's growing body and changing consciousness.

CHAPTER IV

The Map of Childhood

THIS question of whether there are stages in children's lives is of some importance. If there are not, and if every child develops in his own unique way, childhood becomes a nightmare journey for which there is no map.

It would certainly seem as though the comparatively regular development of the first few months disappears as life proceeds. Even in the matter of crawling, standing and walking, there is no slight difference between different children, and later attainments such as reading and counting are achieved at widely divergent ages. Nevertheless, in spite of these individual differences, there is a remarkable amount common to the development of all children. What is common, however—the kind of thing which makes it possible for a Gesell to give a clinical account of different ages—is not so much abilities as behaviour traits and the relationship to life. This is an indication that Nature is interested in processes rather than achievements. Even children with streaks of precocity or genius often remain typical children in the general run of their lives. So unusual a young person as the Arabian traveller and Orientalist, Gertrude Bell, who was reading tomes like Green's *History of England* at the age of ten, was a thoroughly child-like child in the rest of her life.

If there are stages in childhood at which definite new developments occur it is to be expected that they will appear rhythmically; for all life is remarkable for the fact that it manifests in rhythms. Now there are two physical developments in childhood so obvious as to be noticed by everyone—the change of teeth and puberty. Of the former very little notice is taken; about the latter, in our sex-conscious age, an immense amount has been written. It is remarkable that both these important physical changes occur in approximately a seven years rhythm. The seventh year is the great toothless age; while puberty, earlier in girls than in boys (for reasons which will appear later) centres in the fourteenth year. Add to this the old tradition that full maturity comes with the age of twenty-one and you have a threefold rhythm of seven years. Is there any connection between this triple rhythm and the threefold organisation of man described in the last chapter? A Steiner education is built on the belief that there is.

We have noticed the polarity between physical growth on the one hand and the development of personal consciousness on the other. If we endeavour to trace these two processes through childhood we will be struck by the fact that growth proceeds from the head downwards, while the awakening to consciousness—a process for which the word 'awakeness' might well be coined—develops from the limbs upwards. We are right to speak of children as 'waking up'; but we ought really to describe them as 'growing down'. If we remember the radial form of the limbs and the spherical form of the head, we could equally say that the one is centrifugal while the other is centripetal.

To begin with the question of growth, we have the remarkable fact that it is the head which is first formed in the embryo. At birth the brain weighs as much as one-sixth of the entire body, and even in the tenth year the proportion is still one to ten, whereas the adult ratio, which is reached about the age of twenty-one, is only one to thirty-five or thirty-six. It is the disproportionate size of the brain, and consequently of the forehead, compared to the small nose and still smaller chin, which gives a child that air of serene wisdom which he will probably never attain again in his later life. By the seventh year the brain has almost reached its full development. If its size relative to the rest of the body is still so great, it serves to show how slowly trunk and limbs develop. It is an event in the sphere of the head—the change of teeth—which brings the physical development of the head, or more precisely of the upper head, practically to its conclusion.

When the rest of the body begins to overtake the head in growth after the change of teeth, it is in connection with the chest that we notice the first main advance. Not only does the whole trunk grow longer but the rhythmical processes centred in the chest show a marked advance. We find, for instance, that during the middle period of childhood—from the change of teeth to puberty—the pulse slowly reaches the adult rate. Undoubtedly the consciousness of the small child is affected by the high rate of his pulse. The blood courses through the body of a baby nearly twice as fast as with the adult. The vivid perception of colour which comes in a fever may give us some idea of how bright is the world in which a child lives.[1] The pulse remains high in the early years—it is still 100 at the age of ten—but as the rhythmical system is formed and strengthened it gradually lessens and reaches the normal 72 at about fourteen or fifteen.

It is noticeable in these middle years how easily and delightfully rhythm appears in a child's movements. The small child is not originally rhythmical; his movements are even somewhat spasmodic. But from the age of six up to the approach of puberty is an epoch of graceful movement hardly recaptured in later life. Gesell has well noticed the age of six as the time when children are susceptible to the magic of number in rhythmic counting. If a child is obstinate over his food at this age, tell him that he is going to swallow his spoonful when you have reached seven and begin counting rhythmically one . . . two . . . three. With luck you will get him to clear his plate, as every adult knows every good child ought to do. A teacher called from the room can chain his class to their chairs while he is away if he tells them to count to a hundred before he returns, and starts them off in a rhythmic chant. The children instinctively practise rhythmical movement in running, skipping and hopping; and when they recite a poem they naturally emphasise the rhythm and not (as our modern actors do) the sense.

This wonderful rhythmical age disappears as the children approach puberty. The third epoch of youth now begins. Girls' legs grow lank—or sometimes extremely fat; boys shoot up (or rather down), and it is plain where the growth is from the wrists appearing out of sleeves and the ankles out of trousers. The unfortunate younger brothers inherit the still serviceable jackets and trousers. The boys especially cannot cope with the sudden growth of limb, and a spell of clumsiness sets in when everything seems to be in their way. All this goes with the completion of the lower trunk in the development of the sexual organs.

This working of the growth-forces from the head downwards appears in a more limited sphere in the head alone. The head may be called the finished part of the body in which it is easiest to see the whole man in miniature. The whole body in its three systems

[1] Goethe (who was deeply interested in colour) when serving as Quartermaster with the Weimar contingent of the allied forces at the time of the French Revolution, went up into the front line to prove for himself that the so-called 'cannon fever' enhanced the brilliance of colours.

is an expression of the powers of thought, feeling and will, but this expression is repeated on a smaller scale in the head alone. This reflection of the whole in the part is the principle which the Middle Ages called the principle of Correspondences, or of Microcosm and Macrocosm. It is one of much importance for education and will appear again and again in the course of this book. For the medieval mind its supreme example was in the relation of man to the universe. Man was not considered as a mere part of the universe, he was a universe in miniature. His heart corresponded to the sun; the fixed stars of the zodiac formed the different parts of his body—a belief still so common in the sixteenth century that Shakespeare could joke about it in his plays.[2] Animals, plants and minerals all had their part to play in the microcosm of man.

If we view the head from this point of view, we must say that it is only the upper part of the head, containing the brain, which is truly and essentially 'head'. In the lower part of the head we find in the jaws a miniature of the limbs, of which only the lower jaw has the freedom of movement characteristic of the limbs, while the upper has been caught into the rigidity of the head. The jaws are really two pairs of limbs, but each pair has been joined together, as in the clasping of hands, to make the circular form natural to the head nature. It is not entirely fanciful to see in the ten milk teeth of the upper jaw, and the corresponding ten of the lower, something like the fingers and toes of the limbs themselves. In the mouth, again, we find in the flow of the saliva the first beginning of the digestive system—linked to the jaws as intimately as the digestive organs proper are linked to the movements of the lower limbs.

Between the limbs and the head in the whole human body are the central organs of rhythm, heart and lungs. The nose in the head occupies a similar intermediate position between forehead and jaw, and it is in the nose that respiration begins just as diges-

[2] *Twelfth Night*, Act 1, Scene 3.

Sir Toby Belch: Were we not born under Taurus?
Aguecheek: Taurus! that's sides and heart.
Sir Toby: No, Sir, it is legs and thighs. Let me see thee caper.

The joke, unintelligible to a modern audience, is that both are wrong. The constellation of Taurus 'corresponds' with the region of the throat. The allusions to 'correspondences' in Shakespeare are almost countless. They are a principal theme of *The Merchant of Venice*.

tion begins in the mouth. It is interesting to see how much of the life of feeling has always been associated with the nose, and the varieties of moods it has evoked. It is aristocratic or it is plebeian: it is an organ of fine sensibility and, through incense, has its part even in religious devotion, or it provides matter for innumerable witticisms. Cyrano de Bergerac would surely not have felt his plight so deeply if nature had enlarged his chin rather than his nose.

For our present purpose, however, the important thing to notice is that the three parts of the face develop *pari passu* with the whole body. The minute proportions of nose and chin remain throughout early childhood: in the middle period the nose develops: the jaw grows with the limbs in adolescence. A young child with a 'lantern jaw' would indeed be a monstrosity. Nature is consistent with herself and develops the head in conformity with the entire body.

The principle of the 'whole in the part' is also to be found in both the rhythmical system and the limbs, though there it appears more by way of function than of physical form. It is the nature of the head to bring everything to physical expression. A bust reveals the entire man; a torso does not.

While we have to start with the head in examining the direction of growth, we must begin with the limb system in its connection with metabolism if we wish to watch how a child wakes up. It is plain that the first sentient experiences of the new-born child are in connection with his food. His complete devotion to food is not a crude thing as it would be in an adult. He has a spiritual experience in the tasting of his food, which is to him a revelation of spiritual powers as much as the cataracts were to Wordsworth or the song of the skylark to Shelley. There is hardly a more sublime sight than a small child's rapture over his food. It is incredible that some psycho-analysts imagine that this represents 'the cannibalistic phase of development'. How easy it is to plant an erroneous conception of the origin of man into the early history of the child!

The child's delight in food very quickly passes into limb movement, as the ecstatic kickings and stretchings amply testify. It is in the use of his limbs that he first becomes awake to the world.

If we read correctly the signature of the child's body, this activity of the limbs means that he is awake in his life of will.

The will of a small child is phenomenal and needs no labouring. It often makes him the dominant member of the family, especially if he is the only child. In a later chapter it will be shown that all aspects of the small child's life partake of the nature of will, even his first essays in thinking. We need only notice here that when he begins to use his organs of sense-perception his interest is always in the activity they reveal, to which he at once responds with activity of his own. It is the moving object which catches his eye, and his looking is always closely associated with the movement of the limbs. It is not enough for a child to see—he wants to handle and touch. A small child invited to look at an interesting object demanded with exasperation, 'Let me see with my hands.' *Do not touch* is to a child the most desolatory of adult prohibitions.

The absorption of all activity into the sphere of the will produces a wonderful faculty of concentration in the young child. What he does he does with all his mind and all his heart and all his soul. He is never doing one thing and thinking of another. It is this concentration which gives a child's play its distinguishing mark of high seriousness. It is almost a sign of genius if an adult has the same capacity for total application to the task in hand.

Rudolf Steiner was particularly interested in the age at which thinking can first be said to become properly detached from bodily limb activity. He found it to be about the time of the change of teeth, because at this time a double event of great importance is taking place. The growth forces, working from the head downwards have, in a sense, completed the upper head and begin to concentrate more on the central part of the body; while the awakening consciousness, hitherto concerned with the life of the limbs, invades the same middle sphere of rhythmical processes. Hence a life of feeling begins to awaken in the child, and he now experiences the world not so much through the 'sleeping' will-consciousness as through the 'dreaming' consciousness of feeling. Feeling, however, is more detached from the world than willing, though it by no means makes that complete separation of subject and object which thinking does. The will goes directly into contact with the outer world. Feeling can cultivate an inner life devoid of action.

This feeling-consciousness we have already described as essentially pictorial in character, akin to dream-consciousness. It now begins to demand that play of emotion, sympathy and antipathy, joy and sorrow, courage and fear, which is to the soul what breathing in and breathing out are to the lungs and heart.

Naturally a child is not devoid of feeling in his earlier 'willing' stage, but a simple piece of observation will show how great is the change to this new experience. Children of five will be satisfied by a story about very simple activities. You can tell them how the farmer goes out in the evening to feed his animals, and first he goes to his pigs, and then to his cows, and then to his sheep, and so on, and in what language they all thank him and say good night; and then how he comes home and eats the lovely supper his wife has prepared for him and goes to bed himself. The mere picture of the successive actions is a story for these little children. But if you told such a story to children of seven and upwards you would have a very poor reception. For them a story must live in the sway of feeling. There must be a time when the young prince is lost alone in the forest, and night comes and dreadful noises issue from the darkness and there is a flashing of mysterious eyes. Then at last he sees the welcome sight of a cottage with the red glow of a comforting fire shining through the window. At this cottage door the prince must knock seven times (not less than seven times in this age of rhythm) and, when he has almost given up hope, he hears a footstep within and the bolts are slowly drawn. And who is it who at last opens the door? A frightful witch. He turns to run but finds himself rooted to the ground. . . . All this sway of feeling, which would have been meaningless or harmful to the five-year-olds, is the very life-blood of a story to these older children who have passed the threshold of a new experience. For the soul no less than the body now demands its systole and diastole, the contraction of fear and sorrow, the expansion of laughter and hope. What is the reproach uttered by the children in the Bible? 'We have piped unto you and you have not danced; we have mourned to you and you have not wept.' The children wish to play at weddings and funerals, to enjoy both laughter and tears. It is the duty of adults to give them the right opportunities to do so.

Much will be said later about the pictorial quality of a child's thought, which often makes it so inaccessible to the adult mind. A single word in a sentence for some odd reason may suggest a picture to a child's mind which quite obliterates the logical meaning of the words. Piaget gave a number of children a group of those proverbs like 'Birds of a feather flock together' in which our ancestors still expressed their wisdom in pictorial form. At the same time he gave them the meaning of each proverb expressed in general terms and asked them to put together the right meaning with the right proverb. He found that up to the twelfth year they were almost totally unable to make the right association. The associations they made—which they were convinced were correct—were based on some word similarity or fantasy of their own mind.

One other quality of the child's thought at this age must be added. It is essentially uncritical. The child naturally wishes to believe what he is told. He expects the adult to know the answers to his questions and he expects those answers to be true. It is the age of a rhythmical relationship between child and grown-up. The child gives his confidence, and in return he expects to receive wisdom and authority.

This first independent thinking, then, has three main characteristics which distinguish it from later thought. It lives in the sway of feeling, it is pictorial and it is uncritical. In spite of many changes and developments it is essentially thinking of this character which marks the central years of childhood from the change of teeth to puberty. At the latter age a double process occurs, as at the change of teeth, which brings about a new epoch in the child's life.

At about the age of fourteen, as has already been described, the growth forces work especially on the lower trunk and the limbs. But at the same time the awakening powers of consciousness reach the head. The head rather than the heart now becomes the bearer of thinking and all the characteristics of intellectual thought begin to occur. The critical faculty develops with all its good and bad characteristics. The adolescent no longer accepts authority, but wishes to form his own opinions. He is extremely clever and ruthless in argument, and the wise adult will avoid controversy with him. At the same time, in connection with the rapid growth of limb, new will-power manifests itself which he finds hard to control. The rhythmical powers seem unable to hold the balance between thought and will. Judgment will be insecure until the new development is completed towards the age of twenty-one.

To sum up, in the growth of children we have to recognise three principal epochs of development: an epoch of will activity, an epoch of pictorial thinking impregnated with feeling, and an epoch of intellectual thought. The three epochs can naturally be characterised in many different ways. They can also be called the epoch of imitation, the epoch of authority, and the epoch of idealism—only it must be remembered that ideals may be bad as well as good, and even the ideology of the Teddy-boy or the cult of the gangster is a form of ideal. More will be said of the three epochs from this point of view under the heading of discipline. Meanwhile we have brought together the threefold organisation of man with the three epochs of childhood in their connection with physical growth and consciousness. In a map on so tiny a scale—five minutes to twenty-one years—only the principal features can be shown, and no doubt many difficulties and anomalies will have presented themselves. Later chapters on the successive epochs will both clarify and modify this essential picture. But other factors which affect the whole course of childhood must first be considered.

CHAPTER V

Consciousness and Ego-Consciousness

THE three stages of development described in the last chapter are fundamental in the understanding of childhood. Education would not be an easy task if it had to deal with these three alone. But we are not dealing only with faculties such as thinking, feeling and will; we have to reckon also with the emergence of the ego-being in which those faculties are centred, and which in fact calls them to life.

Once we touch the question of the ego, the central unifying power of the human being, we are face to face with the greatest of all the riddles of existence. There is no more difficult command to fulfil than the old Greek exhortation: Know Thyself. Almost the whole history of human thought can be called the attempt of man to obey this command. It is only in modern times that man has imagined he can know the world without knowing himself. Difficult as the question of the ego is, however, it must be faced in any serious work on education. For how shall we know the child without knowing the man?

In many of his writings on the nature of man and of the world Rudolf Steiner discusses the connection between man and the animal kingdom. According to natural science there is no essential distinction, only a gradation, between man and animal. Steiner held the contrary view that there is a difference *in kind* between the two, in that man possesses a principle unknown to the animal—that of ego-consciousness. He pointed to the faculty of *memory* as an essential condition of ego-consciousness.

There is much in the life of higher animals which seems to point to the possession of memory. A dog (like that of Odysseus) recognises its master after many years. If its master dies, it will even pine away and die of grief. Nevertheless it does not remember its master in the proper sense of memory. It does not evoke memory pictures by its own spontaneous activity. Through association the presence of the master becomes necessary to its physical welfare, in the same way as food and drink are necessary. When the master dies or is away, the dog 'starves' for want of him as it would starve for lack of food. All the apparent feats of memory by animals can be accounted for by a similar organic basis. It is through their absence of a 'personal' memory that animals are so much wiser than man in the sphere of instinct. The glory of the animal is not that it has a little bit of what man has in abundance, but that it has so much in its own right. Even of the insects we can say, as Thomas Hardy said of those that came through his window, 'They know earth-secrets that know not I.'

How far back into childhood can memory go? It is an interesting exercise to try to remember as far back as one can. Very few people indulge in the exercise and the average adult can rarely remember anything before his fourth year. Of 200 students in an American college only 22 could remember anything before the age of three but 76 could remember something that happened to them between three and four. It might be thought that memory could go back as far as consciousness. This is not so, however. There can be consciousness without memory. But it is memory which binds together a sequence of experiences as the unique possession of everyone who calls himself by that name which is common to all and yet unique to everybody—*I*.

It is a moment of immense significance when, in learning to speak, a child first calls himself by the word 'I'. Every other word can be learnt by imitation, this word only *through an inner realisation of ego-hood*. Some people can remember the moment in childhood when for the first time they realised that they were not father or mother or aunt or uncle, but—'I'. That mysterious being Kaspar Hauser, who was brought up in a dungeon, without light or human intercourse, until he was released in the streets of Nuremberg at the age of eighteen, provides the rare spectacle of someone going through a kind of early childhood at an advanced age. When his guardian once told him to go and tell someone, 'I want this,' he went and repeated, 'I want this.' When the guardian corrected him, 'No, not you, I,' he passed his hands down his body repeating, 'I, I, I.' For the first time there had awoken in him the realisation which comes to children generally in their third year, that he was an 'I'.

This moment of the first act of self-consciousness is the 'Great Divide', the barrier past which it is rare indeed for memory to penetrate. Probably everyone with sufficient exercise and concentration could reach this point of time in memory. Among those few who claim to have passed it was the seventeenth-century writer Thomas Traherne, who speaks of a world of light in which he was

> All life, all sense,
> A naked simple pure intelligence.

Indeed Traherne exactly describes that ability of the child to enter directly into his environment which is the basis of his imitative powers.

> An Object, if it were before
> Mine Eye, was by Dame Nature's Law
> Within my Soul: her Store
> Was all at once within me: all her Treasures
> Were my immediate and internal Pleasures; . . .

It is small wonder that with such memories of childhood in his mind Traherne wrote: 'Our Saviour's meaning when He said: *Ye must be born again and become a little child that will enter into the Kingdom of Heaven,* is deeper far than is generally believed.' And how Traherne would have approved of Emerson's sentence: 'Infancy is the perpetual Messiah, which comes into the arms of fallen men and pleads with them to return to Paradise.'

Of course, nothing of this will be found in any modern textbook of education. The notion of the ascent of man from primitive forms of life to ever higher and higher stages of consciousness has completely dominated thought in the past century, and a dominant thought operates even at times and in spheres in which it may not be present in the conscious mind. This is why it is assumed by modern educators that childhood is intrinsically a time of learning, and they overlook the fact that it is also a time of forgetting.

Modern analytical psychology attributes immense importance to the state of the psyche in early childhood, and, within the limits of its technique, it has discovered many interesting things about it. Moreover, because childhood is the root of the unconscious and subconscious life, it is the 'uprooting' of childhood experience which is regarded as one of the most fruitful ways of examining the non-conscious mind. Jung, for instance, traces the process by which the descent into the unconscious leads you from the personal to the impersonal, to the 'archetypes' common to all humanity and therefore appearing also in the myths and legends and religions of the entire world. His *shadow* principle is the personal unconscious and includes (among much else) 'all those uncivilised desires and emotions that are incompatible both with social standards and our ideal personality'—in fact, the lower or animal nature in man. Below this he finds in the unconscious a principle of a more universal nature—in the man an idealised feminine being whom he calls the *anima,* and in the woman its male counterpart called the *animus.* Even deeper than this he has discovered an archetype of great wisdom, this time of the same sex, the *old wise man* for the male and the *great mother* for the female.

It is just in this sphere where psychologists are groping today that Steiner's spiritual investigations have so bright a light to throw. For the psychologists find the *personal element* rooted in the impersonal, and in nothing else. Because they have no technique for passing over the 'Great Divide' they do not reckon with the fact that the essential personal element—the ego—is a spiritual entity which has its origin in a spiritual world. In Steiner's view, however, in the conception and birth of a child we are concerned with the interpenetration of two worlds, the physical and the spiritual. The parents mediate into existence the physical body with its life processes, and thereby make it possible for the ego with its individual consciousness to descend from spiritual worlds and implant itself on the earth.

The physical body, however, is the expression of far greater powers of wisdom than any that can be grasped by the individual ego-consciousness. It is described by Steiner as the oldest and most wonderful part of man. Its origin is in a time when matter did not exist in the densified state in which it is found today, before even life appeared in the history of the earth. It may therefore be described as the element which man shares with the mineral kingdom.

The mineral is distinguished from the plant by the absence of inner organic processes. These, in Steiner's view, are not the cause but the result of a life process. It is a life process which permeates physical substance and brings about, for instance, the flow of sap in the plant, and of blood in animal and man. These life forces form the 'life-body' of an organism no less than the physical substances form the physical body. Steiner therefore speaks of a 'life-body' (he also used the term 'etheric body') in addition to the 'physical body'. It is this life-body with its formative powers which creates the essential form of an organism. We have already described it in one of its aspects as the growth force which works from the head downwards in developing the physical body in childhood. We see its work also in the almost magical power of healing, when damaged tissue is restored to its proper form and function.

In many respects the life-body is the polar opposite of the physical body. For example, the physical body obeys the law of gravity and is centripetal in character. But the plant—the first kingdom above the mineral to possess a life-body—raises itself from the ground towards the heavens. It is centrifugal in character.

In another very important respect, also, the life-body is the opposite of the physical. If the one is male, the other is female. If the one is female, the other is male. When Jung speaks of *anima* and *animus* he is really describing the image of woman present in the life-body of every man, and the image of man present in the life-body of every woman, as they live in the unconscious mind. That recovery of the total man which, at its highest, marriage represents, is implicitly present in every individual. Once we realise this, a new wind blows through all those cloudy discussions which have made the name of Oedipus a household word to be heard 'on every infant's tongue'.

If the life-body yields to the dreaming picture consciousness an image of the opposite sex, the physical body naturally produces one of the same sex. Thus, in Jung's 'great mother' and 'old wise man' we have something like a picture of the ancient wisdom built into the structure and substance of the physical body.

In little children—before the advent of memory—some of both these spheres of wisdom are translucent, together with a dim consciousness of the spiritual world from which the yet unconscious ego has descended. Then from the time when he first realises his own individuality the shades of the prison house begin to close upon him, and he loses his participation in the Heaven which 'lies about us in our infancy'. Man sacrifices a great deal in order to become an ego-conscious being.

We can now better understand what has already been hinted at, that Steiner went the opposite way to the psychologists, in that they endeavour to draw what is unconscious in the human being up into consciousness, while he took consciousness down into the sphere of the life-body and the physical body and made them yield up their secrets. What he has to tell about the unconscious, therefore, is not limited to the human psyche but extends to those universal and historical forces out of which both the inherited body and the incarnating ego are born. One outstanding event in the history of mankind he has related to the moment in the child's life when he first says 'I'. For by the principle of 'correspondences' the child's life reflects something of the history of all mankind. This is nowhere more true than in the case of that catastrophic event known to many religious and mythological traditions, but best described in the Old Testament, where it is called the Fall of Man.

The development of ego-consciousness has depended historically on the absorption of the ego in the physical body, by which man has gradually lost his participation in the spiritual creative forces of Nature, and has learnt to view the world as something outside himself (*not-I*) which only reveals itself to him through his senses. The modern conquest of the material earth and its forces is the external sign that the ego is incorporated in physical matter to an extent which has never obtained before.

The Fall of Man has therefore a double aspect—a descent into the experience of the material physical body and the first step in the awakening of ego-consciousness—both of which are clearly characterised in the story of the Old Testament. There is nothing inherently evil in either of these aspects. Why then is the Fall described as the result of the Temptation of Lucifer, the enemy of God? It is because it gave man knowledge and the experience of good and evil before he was adequately developed and could properly sustain it. It is through this that the ego of every man has its 'shadow' side, something of which appears even in early childhood from the first moment of self-consciousness.

Never was it clearer than it is today that through his knowledge man has achieved a power which he is not morally mature enough to wield. This tragic fact lies behind all responsible utterances of our time. To give one example, the President of the British Association for the Advancement of Science in an inaugural address recently diagnosed the *malaise* of mankind in an interesting manner. What is wrong with man, he said in effect, is that his knowledge is heritable, each generation beginning with the stock left by its predecessor: but morality is not heritable, everybody has to begin again at the beginning. We know far more than our forefathers, but we are not better men.

Regrettable as it may seem, this state of affairs is a condition of human freedom. If we inherited a stock of virtue from our parents we should be virtuous by the very fact of that inheritance, without the exercise of our own free will. But we cannot shut our eyes to the fearful picture of almost illimitable power in the hands of almost irresponsible men.

Lucifer gave man knowledge before he was ripe to receive it, when the tree was still forbidden to him. With knowledge came self-knowledge, and freedom to see the better and choose the worse. Man entered into his inheritance of the earth with divine faculties but, through his premature ego-hood, with the ability to use those faculties for selfish and destructive ends. Here is the central Mystery of human life as the Christian must see it. *Christus versus Luciferus*. The Christ, the bearer of Divine Love, redeems the selfish quality in the human ego through the power of love, and the individual becomes 'a law unto himself': but that law is the law of love, which man left behind when he forsook the Garden of Eden to find knowledge and freedom.

It is the microcosmic aspect of this premature ego-consciousness which we encounter in the life of every child. For childhood can be described in almost opposite terms. It is a time of divine innocence, of beautiful imagination, of touching confidence in parents and teachers, of generous recognition of the achievements of others, of devoted interest in the whole world. But it is equally a time of dreadful egotism, of unbelievable cruelty, of fearful destruction, of horrible prurience, of every kind of falsehood and deception.

It is no exaggeration to say that at various times different schools of thought have viewed children in such opposite and extreme colours. The Puritans, with their overwhelming conviction of original sin, often spoke and acted as though they believed that nothing but sinful impulses could exist in the unredeemed child. Later schools of thought—dating perhaps from Rousseau and the cult of the 'noble savage'—have held that the child is all innocence, and corruption only comes to him through the influence of society. So easy it is to see things from one side only.

We have to realise what measure of truth there is in both views. If we think of the faculties of the child, his selfless gift of imitation, his creative power, his intensity of concentration and interest in what he does, we seem to be in an almost divine world. But the tragedy of the Fall is enacted in his little life just as it was enacted in the great history of mankind. He becomes self-conscious before he is mature. Selfishness, jealousy, pride and all the qualities of egotism enter into him. At the moment when he first says 'I' the gates of Eden begin to close upon him.

If we could imagine that there had been no 'Fall', and that consequently the child did not experience ego-consciousness in the immature stage at which it is now born in him, how different would be the task of education! Before he says the word 'I' a child learns three things of immense significance: to walk erect, to speak and to think. These three form the greatest step he ever takes in his whole development. How does he learn these faculties which are the foundation for all he will ever learn in life? Not, assuredly, from human teachers! He learns them from those divine, universal powers which have formed his body and given it life, with which his sleeping consciousness is still in communion. If he did not take the plunge into self-consciousness he would continue to develop under their guidance. But with his dawning sense of ego the child takes his first step on to the earth, and human teachers take over from divine powers the task of guiding him to manhood. That task is a very great one. It is none other than to guide him in such a way that, when he reaches the true age of self-consciousness and self-reliance at the threshold of manhood, he shall receive a self redeemed by the power of love.

It will be the task of later chapters to deal with the impact of the child's ego-consciousness on his growing faculties. In each seven-year period there is a point of enhancement of self-consciousness corresponding to the moment of saying 'I' in the first. In small children the dawning ego-consciousness naturally operates in the sphere of the will. All children go through the stage of rejecting everything that is proposed to them. How they love to say 'No' when you say 'Yes', until it becomes a game of which they never seem to tire. It is a pretty thing to watch this principle of rejection at war with the necessity to imitate. The child will not join in the game and sits sulking on a chair. But his eyes are drinking in all the other children are doing and, if he is left alone, before long he slips from his chair and pushes his way into the circle. But you must not see him, or call attention to him. He must not seem to do the thing which *you* want. Already he is a little person and has 'a will of his own'.

CHAPTER VI

The First Seven Years

THERE is nothing comparable in later life to the development of the first seven years. It is beyond all doubt the chief formative period for the whole of life. Never again do we learn so much, experience so much, or develop so many abilities. It is a favourite and in some ways the most rewarding age for child-observers and psychologists. On the one hand development follows a far more constant pattern than in later years. On the other, the child guards the secret of that development so closely that any number of theories can be woven round the facts observed. His bodily movements we can observe: but he tells us very little about his mind and feelings until half of this first period is over: and even then it needs genius to interpret the fragment of his life he reveals to us, no doubt a small part of that small part of his mind of which he is himself fully aware. The child's mind has indeed become what the Bible was once to warring sectarians—the place where you find confirmation of everything you wish to believe.

In almost any field of study it is possible to accumulate facts to the point at which they become unintelligible. The number of day to day, almost hour to hour biographies of the first years of childhood, the films and sound recordings of every phase of development, would fill a library far bigger than any possessed by a medieval university. Can we discover any master-designs in this confused material?

Let us begin by looking at this first epoch of life from the point of view of the threefold evolution of all childhood, with its ascending and descending processes, which has been described in a former chapter. For we shall find that the principle of microcosm and macrocosm does not apply merely to the physical spatial world, as with the head in relation to the entire body; but larger periods of time also are reflected in the smaller parts of which they are composed. It is only to abstract thinking that time is an abstraction. In reality it is a living process, and in it the relation of the part to the whole is that of 'wholeness' as in a living organism, not the mere multiplicity of the components of the machine.

We have already described the growth forces as concentrated in the head at birth, and working their way through the organism to the first full development of the limbs after adolescence. In miniature we can see these forces following the same course in the first period of childhood alone. How weak are the limbs and metabolism in the first months after birth, when the legs cannot even be straightened and the digestion is attuned only to the mother substance of milk! How sturdy are the legs and how omnivorous the appetite of the six-year-old! And how much has happened, less visible to the eye, in the strengthening and regulating of heart and lung to make this transformation possible! The awakening process, however, which moves counter to the growth forces in the whole of childhood, is also echoed in these first seven years, with the result that in some measure we can watch it reaching the head even in this shorter period. To follow these two processes in their reciprocal movements may help us to visualise the hidden principles with which Nature first sets about her task of maturing the child into the man.

The first two years is the supreme time of the head development. At the age of two the upper head and brain come astonishingly close to their full size in maturity. It has been said that, if the head continued to develop at this pace throughout life, in old age we should all have heads as big as the earth. But it is not in the head that consciousness first begins. On the contrary, during the earlier part of this time the child is completely abandoned to his metabolism. If he is experiencing cannibalistic and sex fantasies as he sucks in his mother's milk, he is certainly a consummate actor. For it is impossible to imagine anything partaking less of the earthly passionate and more of the heavenly contemplative than the countenance of the child in his devotion to his nourishment. It is actually true, and not a mere metaphor, that the child's face expresses heavenly contemplation. For there are spiritual forces working behind and through all material substances, and it is in these that the child still participates as he assimilates his food.

Even the first use of the eyes suggests something of the same process of assimilation. The tranquil intensity of the gaze is so penetrating that you feel that he is taking in and digesting his sense impressions no less than he digests his milk. The habit a baby has of suddenly averting his head after looking earnestly and happily at someone is anterior to the dawning of self-consciousness. He averts his head for the same reason that he pushes away the breast—because he has had all he can digest. Indeed the game, which all babies play, of looking and covering the eyes, and looking and covering the eyes until you think they will never tire of it is nothing more than a 'playing out' of this process of taking in and assimilating.

The other archetypal game in which a baby early indulges is building up and breaking down—or (before he can build himself) throwing down for you to pick up—and he will play it until you are exhausted. This breaking down and rebuilding is precisely the function of metabolism. These first acts of play do not come, as later play does, from an imitation of the surroundings, but are an externalisation of inner experience.

All this lively experience of metabolic processes is intimately linked with the activity of the limbs. For the speed with which the limbs develop is phenomenal. Babies have been known practically to turn themselves over with kicking when five days old. In the third month definite directed activity begins, generally in the form of getting the hand to the mouth. By the sixth month the child will be crawling; by the ninth he will probably have pulled himself upright on his legs. The so-called walking reflex, which occurs in the first few weeks of life when a baby held upright on the floor will make definite strides, shows how marvellously the muscles are attuned to upright walking. But this fades away and has nothing to do with the immense energy of will by which the child goes from swimming on the floor to creeping, from creeping to crawling, from crawling to going on all fours, from going on all fours to pulling himself upright, from pulling himself upright to standing and at last triumphantly from standing to walking. We cannot and should not in any kind of way interfere with this royal progress. We can only watch with reverent amazement the triumphant assertion of the human form.

Perhaps Boëthius had some memory of watching this process in the child when he wrote in his *Consolations of Philosophy* the verses in which he contrasts the upright position of man with the 'fallen' bodies of the animals. 'Only the lineage of man lifts his head on high and stands lightly with upright body; and if thou, earthly man, growest evil in thy mind, thy form itself, in that thy countenance lies in the axis of the heavens, counsels thee to lift up thy heart on high so that thy thought be not weighed down or put under foot, since thy body is raised up on high.'

It is the upright position which makes speaking possible; and it is speaking which makes thinking possible. Of course, a child who for some illness has to lie on his back will also learn to speak. But this is because his body is none the less organised for the erect position. The almost universal order of learning is, standing first, then talking, then thinking. In themselves these three constitute a miniature of the whole process of childhood. Standing and walking is a function of the will, which characterises the first epoch of childhood: speaking (which includes listening) brings us into relation with others—it is in the second epoch that children wish to 'hear about the world': thinking—independent in character—belongs to the third.

Especially in the earliest years it is easy to observe that a child's speaking is essentially a will activity. He practices whole sentences of pure meaningless sounds in his cot: he repeats the words he knows again and again, and gesture nearly always accompanies his speech. Up to the third year the principal use he makes of speech is to name things. When we watch the delight and vigour with which he stretches out his hand—almost his whole body—and ejaculates 'Moo-Cow' we seem to be back in that stage of language described in the Bible when God brought every beast of the field and every fowl of the air to Adam 'to see what he would call them: and whatsoever Adam called every living creature, that was the name thereof'. Not only is it an activity of the child to name the objects in the world; the name embraces also the activity of the object. 'Door' means 'open' and 'shut' as well as an object. 'Moo-cow' means a noise, a colour, a movement and a sensation (perhaps even of fear) as well as a visible animal. Psychologists discuss whether a child is thinking without words when he says: 'Mummy-door' or 'Baby-hat', omitting the words 'open' and 'put on'. But in reality the will activity is contained in the word. A hat is not a mere object any more than a door. It is a Thing-you-put-on. Piaget records many cases of children at a later stage (about five years old) who still thought that 'words had strength'. One boy made the remarkable statement about Boxing: 'I thought it was the word that hit.' A name is, in fact, never a mere name to a small child: it is more like a sentence. So that when later on the child begins to use verbs, adjectives and prepositions, he is not adding something on to nouns. He is breaking down a whole complex of meaning into its parts.

All this use of words naturally posits a measure of thinking. But the thinking is almost entirely devoid of general ideas. Nor does so young a child show much sign of affection. He allows himself to be kissed; and when he kisses back it is an objective operation. 'We do that after breakfast,' said an even older boy when asked for a morning kiss. If a baby brother is born while a child is so young there are not likely to be feelings of jealousy, as often happens when a sibling arrives to an older child. Imitation is still unclouded by feeling, and a child may easily be brought to copy his parents in petting and fondling the newcomer.

It is in these first two years of the child's life above all that the adults who have the care of him should bear in mind how deeply he enters into the little world around him and what it means for him to have people around him worthy of his imitation. It is self-education, not child-education, which is needed at this time. To be strictly truthful, to speak always with love, to make every action as beautiful and harmonious as may be—these are the things that affect the child most deeply. For in learning to walk, to speak and to think he is laying the foundation for all that is true, beautiful and good during the whole of his life. In the ancient Persian religious scripture, the 'Zend Avesta', the soul of the faithful after death is said to take three steps. The first step places him in the good thought paradise: the second step places him in the good word paradise: the third step places him in the good deed paradise. It is the erect position that frees the hands and makes the good deed possible; that frees the mouth from the mere service of the body and makes the good word possible; that frees the head from gravity and makes the good thought possible. This is the measure of man; and this the child achieves in his first two years of life.

During the third year a new stage begins, which is something like a miniature of the whole middle epoch of childhood. To be sure, the child is still fundamentally a creature of activity and will, but this activity reveals a new quality of feeling unknown before. On the one hand bragging and boasting soon begin: on the other he becomes much more demonstrative in his affections and a hug and a kiss have some warmth in them. He learns to say 'I like' and 'I don't like'—a pre-echo of that great period of sympathy and antipathy which comes into its own after the change of teeth. In the fourth year he says 'I love' and proposes marriage to his mother or father or any other recipient of his affections. Happy the child who has a home in which he can say 'I love' to everything and everyone. A parent who wished to find out whether his child of just over three could give a reason for his feelings asked him why he loved his mummy and his daddy. The child gave the delightful reply, 'Because I love everybody.'

That one little sentence reveals what an immense stride has been taken not only in feeling, but also in language and thought since the earlier epoch of naming. The child now gives a reason and uses a general term. He will give a reason easily if it arises out of his will or his feelings, but it is pathetic to see the puzzlement of children when asked to enter into abstract or general ideas at this age—a favourite practice of psychologists on the hunt for the emergence of reason. How delightfully concrete are children's minds! One psychologist records drawing his child of three and a half a series of elephants and with each new drawing impressing on the child's mind the proposition that 'all elephants have trunks'. He then drew one without a trunk: but the child did not continue the syllogism, 'this animal has not a trunk, therefore it is not an elephant': his mind was concentrated on the activity of drawing that particular elephant and he asked: 'Hasn't that elephant got a trunk to draw?' It is a most undesirable thing to endeavour to wake children up to abstract ideas before the time is ripe for them. Reason and cause arise gradually out of the concrete experience of feeling and will.

One other symptom of this age is the immense amount of talking in which a child indulges. One precocious child was found at three years to be using no less than 1,020 words. It is significant that the adjectives and adverbs among these words—182 in all—were nearly all acquired during the third year. For adjectives and adverbs express especially what we *feel* about things. In the first phase of speech the child expressed his relation to things by the simple intonation of the word: now he has acquired a new group of words to express his feelings.

Speech with children is not the mere vehicle of communication into which it shrinks for most adults. It is an activity giving immense delight. The rhythmical element becomes very pronounced. Not only does a child delight in repeating and hearing Nursery Rhymes; he creates his own rhythmical babble as he goes along. He accompanies everything he does with an incessant flow of speech. But Piaget has well noticed that the speech of the child even up to the seventh year is chiefly monologue. When others are present his questions are addressed at large without any expectation of an answer or chagrin when no answer comes. The 'Why' questions, which begin about three, Piaget considers for the most part to express disappointment that something had not occurred or could not be done, and not to be genuine questions at all. He also notices that, if no answer is given by the adult, the child frequently answers his question himself. This questioning and answering has in it something of the same character as the looking and hiding of an earlier year, and most probably has a similar origin. It is certainly entirely wrong for adults to turn the practice into an occasion for developing logical and scientific reasoning even in its most elementary form.

With this growth of feeling comes that dawn of fantasy which shows itself, for instance, in the charming ability, which cannot be sufficiently encouraged, to see likeness in form and gesture. A forked stick becomes at once a man: an acorn cup a saucepan: a coat-hanger a telephone: any object in the house may be seized on and turned into something else; while the child himself becomes a tractor or a tiger or a bird or a fish at will. Some children at this age develop an imaginary playmate. The child does not merely build a castle in the air as he might at a later age; he goes out and actively plays with the character his fantasy has created. His fantasy, too, finds its expression in the energy of his will.

About the age of five the third epoch begins. On the one hand, as the growth forces descend, the legs grow sturdy and the hands stronger and more able. On the other hand, something of the head nature awakens as the crown of his first period of childhood. Many interesting things have been noticed as belonging to this age. The child now begins to ask those philosophising questions which he may well spend the rest of his life answering—except that he will probably lose sight of them altogether in the rush and hurry of business. He asks about God. Who made him? Is he a man? Where does he live? He even criticises God. 'He made a mistake when he made a mosquito.'[1] It is extremely easy for adults to give prosaic and factual answers to these questions. One of the best ways of finding out what kind of answer a child really wants is to tell him

[1] Gesell, in describing the child of five.

you will give him the answer later on, or merely refrain from answering, and see if he will answer himself. Such answers which children give to their own questions are generally full of delightful fantasy, and are conceived in terms of motive rather than cause. For instance, a girl of about six asked: 'What makes the rain go up into the sky?' The adult, who was more used to thinking of the rain coming down, was wondering what to say, when the child announced she knew the reason: 'It's because the angels want to drink.' One is really only qualified to answer children's questions when one shares their outlook and has acquired a little of their gift of fantasy.

Even when he *thinks* about the world, the child does it in terms of motive and activity. Sometimes psychologists have tried to test children's powers of thought by asking them to define things. They have found that the children at this age, in nine cases out of ten, define a thing by what it does or what you do with it. A fork is 'to eat with': a knife 'a thing to put bacon on your fork': a hen 'something that lays eggs for you': a nose is 'to blow': a dream 'to look at the night and see things': and so on. It is manifestly foolish and unkind to ask a small child to define anything. Let him act in dumb show animals and other objects and his genius will be apparent. But the thought element is far more awake than in the year before. It is significant that now for the first time children begin to play at being dead and recognise that others will die. But it is in many ways a stable and harmonious time. Children are conscious of right and wrong and on the whole they like pleasing by doing 'right'. It is the crowning of an epoch. A year later new emotional factors set in and some of the child-like harmony and balance is disturbed.

We have described this first epoch of seven years as the miniature of the whole life of a child, except that during it everything takes on the aspect of will and activity. We have now to account for the fact that it is the change of teeth which marks the transition from this stage of development to another.

In the earliest years the growth forces are concentrated in the head with the result that, relatively finished as are his head and brain at birth, a child is not conscious in the head in the same way as the adult. A most interesting fact about these growth forces is that in a certain cycle of years they transform the substance of the physical body. The fact that this cycle is one of seven years is undoubtedly connected with the seven years' rhythm of the child's development. Physically speaking, a man is not the same at twenty-eight as he was at twenty-one. Naturally the transformation becomes less complete as he grows older and the growth forces weaken, and it is at its greatest in the first seven years. But this is not the only reason why this first change outstrips all other periods in importance. It is unique also in that it is a change from a substance inherited from the parents to a substance built up by the child's own individual forces.

Steiner attached great importance to this first transformation of substance, both for the child's body and his mind. For there is a struggle in childhood between what the child inherits from his parents and what he brings into the world as his own personal identity or ego. In saying this we are touching on one of the most important aspects of human evolution.

In the early history of man the inherited forces were all important and the individuality hardly emerged from the tribal or family group. In ancient India you accepted the *dharma* of your caste; in Egypt you followed your father's trade or profession; even to this day a family consciousness lives in the East to an extent unknown in the West. But in the modern Western world it is the principle of individuality which has increasingly evolved. It is through this principle that Western man has abolished serfdom, established democracy, broken down the inequalities of sex, overthrown social traditions—and now finds he does not know on what he is standing.

In the life of the individual the battle between heredity and the ego can often be plainly seen. A strong personality sets a stamp on his own features, and the likeness to the family recedes into the background. Sir Thomas Browne, the author of the *Religio Medici* and a sensitive physician if ever there was one, regarded the appearance of the family image on the features of his patients as a sign of approaching death. The individuality was already withdrawing, and the tide of inherited forces was coming in for its last flood. Children themselves have a kind of instinct today that they should become individuals. A healthy child will always feel a certain embarrassment when the well-meaning visitor tells him 'how like he is to his father'.

A most important step in the establishment of a strong individuality is the overcoming of inherited forces through the proper transformation of the physical body by the growth forces in the first seven years. Nature has provided that during these early years the bones shall remain so soft and pliable that even they can be transmuted. There is only one part of the child's body too hard and calcined to be transformed—the milk teeth. With the teeth therefore Nature goes about her task in another way, by discarding them and substituting others built by the child's own forces of growth. But when the adjustment between the inherited forces and what is individual in the child is not well made, the struggle often manifests itself in an unsuspected way. The numerous children's diseases of an eruptive kind, such as measles, where it can be seen that some inharmonious element is working its way out through the skin, are in fact an attempt of the organism to eject unwanted forces of heredity. It can often be noticed in a child who has been making slow progress in general development that after an attack of measles or the like a remarkable advance is made. We do not do the best thing for children when we adopt measures to prevent them from getting these illnesses which are really part of the healthy process of growing up. Apart from such measures of non-interference with Nature it would seem that so deep-seated a growth process was beyond our conscious control. The child's mind, however, is in our hands, and it is not a matter of indifference to his powers of growth what we do with his mind. We must therefore consider the importance of the change of teeth for the development of the child's psychic life. It is at such nodal points as this that we can see most clearly the intimate relation between body and mind.

The formative growing force, which builds the child's body not only in the image and stature of a man but also in the likeness of parent or grand-parent, is plainly an image- or picture-bearing force. Like all invisible powers which express themselves in physical substance, it has its special relation to certain parts of the body, glands, genes and the like. But it is as ridiculous to think that the substance of a gene contains the contour of a cheek, the breadth of a shoulder, or the shape of a foot as it is to imagine that the seed actually contains the flower—colour, geometrical form, texture and all. The growth force is plainly the bearer of an ideal picture or image which in the process of time it mediates into the world of space and matter, the seed and the embryo being its point of entry into that world. In our own experience we can only compare it to the picture-idea with which an artist approaches his material, and to which he gradually gives physical expression.

The comparison is actually more than a mere analogy. For there is another image-bearing force in man in addition to the force of growth. Thought is also a bearer of images, a pictorial force. In its origin thought was entirely pictorial and it is only with the course of time that 'abstract' thought has slowly arisen. Language today is full of 'dead' metaphors—words which once evoked a pictorial experience but have now entirely lost their living creative force. But in its first appearance both in the child and in the human race, thought is a picture-bearing force.

Why is there this strange similarity between the growth force and the earliest form of human thought? It is because the two forces are the *same force operating in different spheres*. In the first cycle of life this force is chiefly concerned with the upbuilding of the body and the transformation of inherited into individual substance. It is only when this task is completed at the change of teeth that it is released from its organic function to become the force of picture-thinking and of memory.

There is by nature a great, though subtle, distinction between a child's consciousness before the change of teeth and his consciousness afterwards. Before that age the child lives in a stream of picture and memories which are working on him almost as part of the growth forces: it is only afterwards that he begins to master and direct them. The difference is subtle and is therefore often overlooked, but it is immensely important. An example may make it plainer. Children of four and five have been known to repeat, sometimes while holding a book (upside down) and pretending to read it, a story of some length practically word for word. But when asked to repeat the effort later on, nothing was remembered. The memory was not under the child's control; it was just part of the stream of life and growth in which he was living.

It lies in the power of the adult to develop mental habits in a child either earlier or later. He can, if he so wishes, make the child conscious and develop his thinking and his memory at a very early age. If he does so, he will certainly narrow the scope of his mind even if he trains it to much acuteness in a limited sphere. We are here concerned, however, with the effect on the growth forces of a child. These will necessarily be weakened if they are taken away from their proper task of forming and transforming the body; and in some respect or other it will be found that the organism is impaired. Such a weakening will probably not show itself until late maturity. For just as memory binds together the extremes of life, so it will be found that a weakness implanted in early life comes to fruition well into maturity.

Every epoch of history has its characteristic diseases, and it is certainly a characteristic of our age that sclerotic diseases and the unnatural growth we call cancer have become so widespread. These diseases are a sign of the fact that the life forces have been weakened in an entire civilisation. There are, no doubt, many reasons for this; but not the least of them is that the growth forces are not allowed their natural development in early childhood.

With the change of teeth we have reached the age at which the first independent forces of thinking are properly released from the growing organism. It is a very happy thing that in America the old tradition is observed that formal schooling does not begin until the seventh year. England is not so fortunate in that respect, and the working of the new Education Act is such as to throw the shadow of examinations right down into the kindergarten. But Gesell is right when he says that the child of the seventh year is not trying to perfect his abilities of the previous year—'Nature is adding a new cubit to his stature.'

CHAPTER VII

The Small Child at Home and School

THE most important thing, both for parents and teachers, is to have the right feeling for a child; and this feeling can only arise out of a true understanding of all that happens in childhood. What you do with a child at any particular time will then spring spontaneously out of the situation, and not be dictated by 'principles' which, like all general rules, seem so often to make nonsense of the particular case. When parents come and ask educational specialists what they shall do in special difficulties with their children, how often it is apparent that the real need is that they should change themselves, and that without this change no suggested line of conduct will succeed. Nevertheless, it may be helpful, by way of illustration, to draw attention to some of the more important practical consequences which must follow from the conception which has been developed of the first seven years of childhood.

A child is born out of the darkness of the womb; he spends most of the early months of his life in the darkness of sleep; he is still virtually a part of his mother even after his birth. He has to be awakened to the light of the day and to the fact of his independent existence. The waking should be as gentle as possible, or we shall disturb that lingering connection with the heavenly worlds which is of such importance for the child's life.

Practically all modern children are awakened too quickly, and generally in the name of hygiene. They are washed the minute they are born, and the process is repeated at frequent intervals: they are exposed to light: in maternity hospitals they are often taken away from their mothers except for stated feeding-hours; the father who visits is only allowed to see his child through a glass window: and, as the child is supposed to be impervious to sound, wireless may be left on for the benefit of the nurses all day long. Even where more natural conditions prevail the influences which have penetrated modern homes in the form of wireless and television, and the conditions of modern life, which compel parents to take their children about in their cars where formerly they would have left them in the nursery, all tend to awaken the child prematurely. It is small wonder that psychologists observe so many fears in children. Gesell, for instance, finds constant fears at all ages from two to seven. Five is the only age he describes as not fearful—but five and a half again becomes very fearful!

Much of this would be avoided if in the first months and years children were protected from premature awakening influences. The new-born child should be disturbed as little as possible; he should be protected from bright light and loud sounds: he should always be near his mother, for a common force of life is still enveloping them both. If at all possible he should be born at home so that he does not have to leave the place of his birth for at least the first three months of his life. As he becomes active it is important to let him take his own time and not to stimulate him in grasping or looking or crawling. It is equally important not to try to advance his talking, not to keep encouraging him to say the names of things but to leave him to his own tempo. What he needs is that the adults, whose talk he hears and imitates, should speak clearly and beautifully and with affection. For the child is as sensitive to the mood as he is to the sound of the tones around him. The impersonal voice of radio and gramophone is not what he needs to imitate. A mother's singing, however poor, is far better for her baby than the best of records. Gesell discovered that up to the age of seven children preferred the gramophone to the wireless. The reason he gives is that they could see it work and *have the same tune over again*. He does not mention any comparison between the gramophone and the mother's own singing—no doubt for the pathetic reason that so few mothers today do sing to their children. Unhappy children who can only choose between the mechanical gramophone and the mechanical radio!

As they reach the third year—the beginning of the middle period of this epoch—and need a greater variety of toys and objects to play with, it is important to see that the things they have about them are beautiful and imaginative. So many picture-books contain nothing but ugly caricatures of men and animals; so many toys are hideous to the eyes and hard and cold to the touch. The toys should always be such as to bring the child's limbs into activity—not objects for him to observe. A wooden engine that he can push about is far better than a model clockwork train. Indeed his instinct is often healthier than his parents' choice, and he will push his clockwork engine along even during the short time while the works are still unbroken. It is better also for toys not to be too finished. For the dawning fantasy is always pretending things to be what they are not, and a realistic doll or a perfect model house leaves no room for something to be added by the imagination. Adults have often been amazed that a child still prefers the old featureless doll with one eye and a leg missing after he has been given a brand-new one which opens and shuts its eyes and has all its joints articulated. A lot of odd shaped pieces of wood—coloured if possible—which can turn at will into fishes or trees or rabbits or Red Indians stimulate the imagination far more than the conventional box of building bricks. What a delight it is to see children in a wood making a palace out of sticks and leaves and grasses and moss. How they love everything they can pull about and form and mould, sand and clay and 'disgusting mud' and the soft wax pulled fearfully from under the hot flame of a candle. The very feel of natural substance is different from the compositions and plastic materials out of which so many toys for children are made today. The adult can educate himself in a new aesthetic appreciation of substance, a fresh sense of form and gesture in the objects around him, if he will get down on the floor and really play with his children.

The child will always play with what comes to his hand. Take him to a place where there is a magnificent panorama and he will pick up some old box or can on the ground and concentrate all his attention on that. He does not need large spaces. A small garden is a park, a mound an Everest to him. How many people who have moved from their homes as children remember garden-paths like turn-pikes and lawns like prairies, and can hardly believe their eyes if ever they revisit the scenes of their childhood! A child would often prefer to play in the garden rather than to be taken for the grand expedition his parents plan for him. It would certainly be better for him.

Even from the beginning of his life a religious parent will say a prayer for his child every night; from about the third year a child will begin to join in, and it will soon become a nightly ritual. It can be a very simple prayer in which the child speaks of the presence of God in his father and mother and friends and in all the world around him: and—because this is the age at which some fears often begin, especially fears of the dark—it is good for the prayers to speak of the protective power of God's love. There is a delightful tale told of a child whose mother had threatened him that Wee Willie Winkie would come for him if he did not go to sleep. 'No, he won't,' the child retorted, 'because I'm in bed, and God is in bed with me!'

The value of such a prayer in giving confidence to a child in his new life is incalculable. But it will not be right to say it—indeed it will be ineffective—unless the parent can himself believe in it. There is nothing worse for a child than falsehood and insincerity in the adult. But if a child can really feel that 'God is in bed with him' when he is small, he will be strengthened in character for the whole of his life. Similarly, the saying of a grace before each meal will make an immense difference in the child's attitude to his food. There is much discussion among educators as to whether you can teach children morals without religion. It is certain that you cannot teach them those feelings of reverence and gratitude from which morality ultimately springs without the religion of a God who 'cares' for his creatures. No man—and certainly no child—can feel gratitude to a First Cause, or a Life Force, or a Principle of Evolution. A child knows the joy of being alive, which most adults forget: everything in the world is a gift to him, and it is natural and proper that he should express his gratitude to the Giver. We must remember also that as yet there is nothing for him in the world which can properly be called evil. He brings with him to the earth the instinct that everything is good. As with St. Francis, Sun and Moon and Water and Fire are his brothers and sisters. See him hold out his piece of biscuit to you with his wonderful instinct of generosity; but when you have taken it and pretended to eat it, he again holds out his hand to receive it. For he treats physical things as though they followed a spiritual law, that the more you give the more you shall receive. Fairy-tales also tell us of the cup which never empties and the wallet of good things which is always full. Love is not consumed but replenished by the giving.

As the child approaches the age of five and the first forces of what may be called conscious thought begin to appear, he will probably be ready for Nursery Class or Kindergarten. But he will still want many things from his parents: stories at night, answers to his questions, help with his play. In one way this age can be compared to adolescence; at both ages it is terribly easy to think that the children are more mature than they are. Even fairy-stories for this age should still be the simpler ones which do not awaken too much thinking or too deep a sway of feeling. When the children ask 'What for?' and 'Why?', try to think in their terms and answer with that kind of fantasy of which examples have already been given. If a child asks, 'Why do the trees take off their coloured leaves at Christmas?' do not give scientific explanations. For the answer given to herself by a child who asked this question was not at all scientific. She said, 'It's because they want God to give them a white dress for the birthday of Jesus.' When a child still thinks of the world in terms of personal motive and personal value, let us refrain from waking him up to impersonal causes and mechanical forces. If a question is asked which you cannot readily answer, tell the child that he has asked a very hard question and you will tell him a story about it later on. You will then have time to think about it: or—if you are lucky—he may answer it himself.

This is a great question age, and many children now ask their parents: 'Where do I come from?' They generally receive the banal answer: 'Out of your mother's body'—and the parents pat themselves on the back for being modern and frank. It is an answer entirely devoid of imagination, and false by implication. For why should we assume that a child is thinking only of his physical body when he says 'I'—an assumption which perhaps only the modern age could have made? Children are often wiser than their parents and tell them that they came 'out of the sky'. Here is an exercise in fantasy indeed in answering such a question. Many fairy-tales have beautiful pictures of the soul descending from heavenly worlds in quest of a body. And is there not the supreme example of the Gospel story in which God himself enters into his mother's womb?

As the children get older and stronger, and can do more damage both to property and to themselves, parents can easily come into direct conflict with them, and a battle of wills often ensues. The fourth and fifth years generally bring this state of affairs to its peak, and it is often a comfort for parents to know that a more docile age is ahead, which will no doubt have its own difficulties but not this particular one. It helps a great deal if the parent will remember that the whole of a child's life is in his will, and that, if he is checked in what he wants to do, the entire light of life goes out. He cannot console himself with hopes, or memories, or comparisons, or sublimations. It is no doubt often necessary to say an emphatic NO; but it is equally important to develop the habit of thinking of every situation positively. If your child wants to play with a sharp knife, do not simply refuse him but ask him to bring something he can cut (it does not matter from how far away) and show him how terribly sharp the knife is. Above all, even if you have only a very little time, even if you are very tired, make a point of *doing* something with him every day. Do not forget that when you sit reading a newspaper you are (in the child's eye) an offence to God and man. You have legs and hands, and are not profiting by them. Get up and create a game. It is far from easy, but the home demands resource no less than business or war. It is your responsibility that the child is there.

* * *

The Nursery Class is a very modern development in education. Former ages were content to leave the youngest children in the care of the home. Even the Greeks, who were public-minded if anyone ever was, did not practise any public instruction till the seventh year. In the rise of the Nursery Class we must therefore to some extent sadly recognise the decline of the home. The large families—with a new child always coming up—the spacious rooms and large gardens which we associate with the prosperous classes of past centuries, were no doubt an admirable soil for the first shoots of childhood. But life was kinder in one respect even to the poorer children. It offered them far more to imitate. Men worked with their hands both in town and country. Even in the town, all but the main streets were safe to play in: and some itinerant tradesman—tinker, knife-grinder, chair-mender or the like—with a group of children round him was a daily spectacle.

Anyone who was a city child fifty years ago will remember the fascination of watching a gang of men breaking up the road surfaces, with the rhythmical sequence of their sledge-hammers always falling with unerring accuracy on the head of the cold chisel. How different from the modern vibratory road-breaker, the very din of which shatters you as you pass! What a contrast of movement between a child imitating the driver of a team of horses—tugging at the reins, lashing out with his whip and shouting encouragement (or abuse)—and the child clinging to a toy steering-wheel and imitating the noises of the gears. A modern child does not often see a man bringing his limbs into full activity in the course of his daily work. There is probably a greater difference in the experience of childhood between now and fifty years ago than between fifty years ago and ancient Rome or Babylon. The small family, the small house, or smaller apartment or flat, the finished product wrapped in cellophane, the death-dealing roads, the chance (and hence the need) for the mother to work—these have changed the child's world. The Nursery Class has to make good the loss of a civilisation.

Small children are not social beings. If you arrange a party for children of three or four each child will take a toy into a corner, and you will be lucky if not more than two want the same toy and the same corner. Piaget found that in the 'Maison des Petits' where he made his observations children worked (or played) alone up to the age of five: then until seven and a half in groups of two but in a transitory way: only after that age was there any real desire to work together. Gesell also finds children playing in fluid groups of two or three at the age of five: but he states that life would be easier for the child if he had to adjust himself *only* to teacher or *only* to parent. None of this seems to offer a very sound basis for a *class* of small children! Negatively, it means that children should, if possible, be kept at home even at the cost of great sacrifices—at least until their fifth year. Positively, it means that the Nursery Class should be as little like a school and as much like a home as it can be made.

The best Nursery Class teacher is therefore the one most able to create the atmosphere of a home—perhaps ideally some mature, even old, person who has brought up her family and through a rich experience of life has achieved that serenity of soul which so often spells the happiest relation between grandparents and grand-children. Nor need that teacher necessarily be a woman. There are many men—even retired men—who have a wonderful way with small children. When Robert Owen, that interesting industrialist who pioneered in so many fields in the early nineteenth century, founded a school for the children of his workpeople, he made an interesting choice for the teacher of his Nursery Class. He had noticed an old factory hand who always had children at his coat-tails and who generally produced something from his pocket to amuse them. He could neither read nor write, but Owen made him the teacher of the youngest children—and with complete success.

When one day it is realised how important for their future life are the teachers of young children, such good and virtuous persons will almost be constrained, like Plato's Guardians, to take up the high office of caring for the very young. Meanwhile it is a commentary on our understanding of childhood and on our civilisation that teachers in High Schools and Universities are considered far more important (and of course receive far better pay) than teachers of children in the most impressionable years. The economy of a Waldorf School considers them of equal value.

It is evident from the nature of the age that a lot of the time in a Nursery Class must be spent in free play. It is here that it can be a model for all parents in providing artistic toys which bring the limbs into the freest and healthiest movement. Many modern toys and much kindergarten apparatus tend to constrain activity and imprison fantasy. This is true of all those toys where parts have to be carefully fitted together: of jig-saw puzzles where the pieces have no connection with the form or colours of the picture: and of all apparatus made to teach children an operation artificially which they could learn by some real activity. If they are to hammer, let them hammer in order to make something and not merely knock pegs into holes: if they are to saw let it be something they can afterwards use or play with.

The toys should not only be such as to stimulate free activity, they should be full of fantasy in their shape and delightful in their colouring. A boat in which two children can rock can be like a dream-ship: a climbing-frame need not be a mere piece of scaffolding but can be full of surprises like a real tree: rocking-horses will rock just as well if they are not realistic: and a little house, with a door into which the children can go and windows through which they can stick their heads, can as well be like the cottage in *Hansel and Gretel* as resemble a modern pre-fab. It is the fantasy element which is so often lacking in modern equipment, even when it provides excellent opportunity for the child's activity.

Much can be done with the layout of even a small garden. Little paths that twist and turn and join and divide: a mound with paths to run up and down: a bank to jump off: a fallen tree: bushes to hide behind and gallop round: a wooden stile or two to climb over: a dark place between hedges where you might meet a dragon—all these supply something which the normal swing and slide and climbing-frame completely lack. It is not that these last should be omitted or neglected: but it is as important to think of the muscles of the soul as of the body, and children hunger for something that helps them to pretend, some quality on which their fantasy can feed.

It is not enough for children to spend all their time in free play. Indeed beyond a certain point they would become restless and bored if left to their own devices. They need something and somebody to imitate. They do not spontaneously make a social group; but if an adult starts an activity they all begin copying and find themselves happily working at the same task side by side. There are so many things the children can do: kneading dough for cakes and all sorts of simple cooking: sewing stuffed dolls and animals: sweeping and dusting and washing up: digging the soil and planting seeds and bulbs—all the things in fact that a child would see done and wish to imitate in an active household. It must be borne in mind that the natural way in which these young children learn is by looking and imitating—not by systematic instruction. To 'teach' them things at this age is to kill that gift of spontaneity which it is so important to carry into later life. Nevertheless it is good sometimes to take them to see even activities that they cannot yet imitate—spinning and weaving on hand-looms, the making of pots, a carpenter or a plumber at work, a gardener pruning the fruit-trees. For children should always be helped to realise what a lot there is they cannot yet do. To tell them, 'You will be able to do this when you are older', confirms their sense of growing up.

One of the most important tasks of a Nursery Class is to prepare the children by rhythmical movement and painting and modelling for the age of artistic expression which they will so soon reach. It is most important that all this is done in such a way that the children are left free to imitate. If they are trained to be over-conscious of their limb movements, for instance—as they often are in schools of dancing—the forces of thinking may well be dulled at a later age. If they are made to colour pictures already drawn in outline, and sometimes even with the required colours indicated, or to colour formed patterns in regular sequence, they will find it difficult when they are older to think in terms of the free play of colour, perhaps even to visualise the free creative working together of other forces in life. The popularity of the word 'pattern' in individual behaviour and social life may be partly due to the fact that so many adults today were taught in terms of patterns when they were very young.

Children should think of colours as living and active entities. Water colours already mixed in jars flow most easily, and all the better if the paper is large and has been slightly damped beforehand. It does not matter if one child covers his paper entirely with red and another with blue—this is a mere matter of temperament—they feel the flow of colour as they put it on. Nor need the children necessarily be painting *something.* If they spontaneously declare what the picture 'is', well and good, though they will often change their mind when they see some new form emerging. But the adult only worries them if he is always asking *what* they are painting. 'You grown-ups want to know everything,' one child is recorded as exclaiming on such an occasion. 'That's greedy of you.' Nothing elaborate should be attempted. It is enough if the children come to love the three primary colours of red and blue and yellow, and to realise through working with them how very different they are.

Modelling should be dealt with in the same sort of way. Real modelling clay is a healthier substance to the touch than artificial mediums, but it must be worked to the right consistency or it will be too hard for the fingers. As the children work—each with his big fat lump on a board—some shape will arise which suggests this or that. But it will quickly turn into something else, and that in its turn will be flattened out, and the process begun again. Meanwhile the teacher is quietly modelling some simple form, which has perhaps the gesture of a cow or a deer or a gnome, but is not too realistic. Sometimes the children will like their models to be kept so that they can play with them, but generally most will go back into the bin for another day. It is the activity which matters.

Singing and Singing Games will play an important part in the Nursery Class. It is also possible in a very simple way to begin Eurhythmy, a new art of movement developed by Rudolf Steiner. As Eurhythmy can profoundly affect education a special chapter must be devoted to its nature and use. All that can be said here is that it is movement both to music and to speech. The children can therefore act a simple story with movements taken from the very sounds of the words: but here again they must be quite free to copy the movements in their own way. Story-telling—another important element—will easily lead to acting. At a later age it is good for children to retell stories; but at this time it is not right to call on the forces of memory which are not yet freed from the forces of growth. But in acting a story children will often spontaneously remember a speech or a rhyme or a charm which came into it. They remember in the will. It must never be forgotten that with children the same thing can be repeated again and again. They are not always craving for novelty like their parents. They even like a story repeated in precisely the same words and will correct the teller if a variation is made. This very repetition is in itself an exercise for the will.

Rhythmic repetition must be found in the ordering of the day. When the children have all arrived, the morning should open with a prayer and some singing, perhaps with the telling of 'news', so that a child who has something of vast import to impart—a fire, or the birth of a baby, or the arrival of kittens—may relieve himself of his burden and enjoy his importance. Then will come the main activity of the day—one day painting, another modelling, another acting and so on. Next will probably come the interval for the mid-morning lunch, which cannot be done with too much graciousness and ceremony, including the saying of a grace. After this the children will scatter for free play, indoors or out. It is quite sufficient if the children can come only in the mornings. If social conditions make it necessary for them to stay in the Nursery Class all day, arrangements will have to be made for meals, resting, etc. But the balance of life then shifts too strongly from the home to the school. Even the best Nursery Class cannot be a substitute for the quietness, security and personality of a home.

At a later age children sometimes like to keep their home and school lives separate. They will even resent it if parents inquire too persistently into what they are doing at school. But in the Nursery Class age there is no such longing for a private life. On the contrary it is important at this age that a child shall feel the greatest unity between home and school. This does not mean that parents should embarrass the Nursery Class teacher by hanging about the Nursery Class all day: but the child should know that what happens in the Nursery Class is considered important at home, and what happens at home is taken notice of at school.

There is one aspect of life where a co-operation between home and school can be particularly effective, not only in the Nursery Class age (though the foundation should be laid then) but also throughout the whole of school life. Children have a far keener perception than most adults of the changes in the seasons. The finding of the first spring flowers, the colours of the autumn, the white miracle of snow, the glory of midsummer days—all these affect them as intimately as the air they breathe and the food they eat. In days when men lived closer to nature these rhythmical changes in the year were crowned by seasonal festivals of a religious kind. Children still need such a religious experience of the year. Here is a whole field of activity which the modern small home cannot undertake alone, but in which parents can fully co-operate with the school. Religious differences need not arise, because the religion of young children is essentially a nature religion. At Easter they all rejoice in the resurrection of new life, the rolling away of the stone from the grave of winter, long before they have any understanding of the Christian Mystery. At Christmas (which was the festival day of all the old Sun religions) they all feel the wintry silence out of which new light is born for the world. There is no lovelier sight than to see children making baskets and nests of flowers and eggs for an Easter Festival, or walking at Christmas along a path marked by green boughs strewn on the floor, each with his candle in his hand to present them to the Sun-Child in the darkness of the midwinter night. The festivals which have survived from older times have become commercialised, orgies of spending and present-giving and eating and drinking. The child needs more than this. Civilisation needs more than this. If the Nursery Class nourishes the soul of the child by giving him a spiritual experience of the rhythms of the seasons, it is also feeding a starving world.

CHAPTER VIII

The Heart of Childhood

THE seventh year has always been considered highly important in the history of education. At this age in Hellas the child issued from the women's quarters and was conducted by the pedagogue through the crowded streets to the school. At about the same age in medieval aristocracy he joined the household of some great lord and entered on his seven years' service as a page to run errands and pick up courtly manners and good breeding. Seven years later at adolescence he became a squire, an age when his humbler contemporary was being bound ''prentice', or perhaps going to the university for his preliminary seven years' course. In former ages there was an instinctive feeling for the importance of the seven years' rhythm in human life, and it was recognised that at the seventh year a child could be educated in a way that was formerly impossible or undesirable. It is modern thought which has tended to abandon the idea of stages of growth marked by the birth of new faculties.

Great as are the alterations between the change of teeth and puberty, there is a coherence in these middle seven years, a thread of more than one strand which holds together the diverse characteristics of a period of great physical, mental and emotional growth. It will therefore be well to review the nature of the period as a whole before examining the variety and change within it. It is a specially important period because the forces of growth and the forces of 'awakeness' are meeting each other in the central rhythmical system—that system which we have seen is both a bridge and a barrier between the head system and that of the limbs. The former, which have brought the head to so high a plastic development in the first seven years, now become specially active in the rhythmical processes of the body: the latter, which have given the child his active life of will up to this age, now begin to endow him with all those qualities of feeling and imagination which rest on the rhythmical life in man. All the forces of the heart, physical and psychical, now come into play. It is a period which may well be called the heart of childhood.

It is an age of free rhythmical movement. Jumping, skipping, hopping, swinging their legs as they sit on the high adult chairs, running as naturally as they walk, the children exercise their rhythmic powers in almost everything they do. When they recite, they naturally emphasise the rhythm (as indeed most poets have done) more than the adult considers seemly. When they sing, it may not yet be in perfect pitch, but you will rarely hear them lengthening out the tune in their own time, as smaller children do and as Sir Roger de Coverley lengthened out the psalms in church. Greek education was much concerned with developing these rhythmical powers. Gymnastic exercises of a rhythmical character, lyre and flute playing were a principal part of the curriculum in the Greek school. The Greeks would have regarded any exercise which was not rhythmical in character as barbarous and inhuman. Our common Western ball-games would certainly have fallen under their condemnation. When in Homer's *Odyssey* the Princess Nausicaa and her maidens played at ball on the beach (after washing the family laundry) they sang as they tossed the ball to and fro—they were, in fact, playing a singing game. Our modern girls do not sing at netball or hockey, nor our boys at football and baseball.

We cannot today revive the Greek form of education; but we can introduce as much rhythm as possible into our homes and schools. This naturally involves singing and playing of instruments, getting by heart and reciting, as well as moving to music. Whatever instrument he may subsequently play, it is good for every child to begin with a recorder or small flute; for in a wind instrument there is the closest of all connections through the breath itself between the rhythmical system and the music. But rhythm means a great many other things as well. It means that both the single day and the whole year shall be full of rhythmical repetition. Children love the same thing to be repeated in the same way and at the same time. Every teacher called on to take a strange class in an emergency knows how indignant it becomes if he does not follow the customary rites. Regular meal-times, regular bed-times, regular tasks at home and school—this is the backbone of a healthy and happy childhood. Educators are sometimes afraid that too much repetition will produce the 'cake of custom'—the law of the Medes and Persians which altereth not—and so stifle originality. But this is to neglect the changing character of each age. Because a small child imitates he will not go on imitating when he is an adolescent; because he loves repetition at one age, he will not continue repeating for ever. On the contrary, repetition at this age (and to some extent in all ages) is an exercise of the will and strengthens those very qualities on which initiative will later depend. It is the intellectual who tires of repetition; it was the intellectual age which abolished the old ritual forms of religion and substituted the sermon and the impromptu prayer. Today every drama must have a new plot, every detective novel display some fresh tricks of ingenuity. But something of former ages still lives in children, when the seasons brought round their customary festivals, songs and plays. They look forward to the return of the same events as the year comes round, the same carols and the same play at Christmas, in which the story of the Birth in the stable is always the same and yet ever new. Until childhood lost its own traditions there were always seasonal games, a season for marbles, a season for tops, a season for hoops or kites. In the marble season no-one would look at a top, nor at a hoop when kites were in.

Important as these things are, there is a more subtle aspect of the rhythmical life which is little regarded in education today. All rhythm—not only that of the heart and lungs—is intimately involved with a process of breathing in and out. Every day is a time of the inbreathing of new experiences: every night a time of surrendering in sleep what has been won for good or ill during the day. Every year brings the contracting process of winter, when life sinks into the depths of the earth: and the expansiveness of summer, when it soars with the pollen into the far spaces of the atmosphere. Human life itself swings from the inbreathing of childhood and youth to the outbreathing of old age: it is bounded by the inbreath at birth which brings the first experience of the earth and the outbreath at death which carries the departing spirit into other worlds.

When Rudolf Steiner spoke to the teachers of the first Waldorf School he once characterised their task as *teaching the children to breathe properly*. By this he did not, of course, mean that the teachers should give the children actual breathing exercises, but that they should so arrange the course of the day and the form of each lesson that there is a continual interplay between the breathing in of new experiences and the breathing out of will activity.

How do we best prepare children for the nightly breathing out of the spirit into the world of sleep? Not, assuredly, by giving them exciting experiences before they go to bed or by stimulating their thought life through late homework. The first part of the morning is the time for children to breathe in new thoughts and ideas, for them to become awake in the sphere where consciousness chiefly resides—in the brain and intellect. Then should come rhythmical activity, singing, eurhythmy and the like; and, finally, to crown the school day some healthy occupation with the hands and body, craft work, carpentry, or gardening. Thus the child uses all his powers in the right sequence during his day at school and is well prepared for the more spontaneous activity at home. Happy the child in these modern days for whom it will be activity and not an evening of sitting before the television screen. The active hobby may be more trouble to the parent, but is far better for the child. If children have to be helped to find home activities today, it is no doubt partly due to social conditions; but it is often also a sign that something has been killed in their younger years. Tom Sawyer and Huck Finn had very little difficulty in occupying their leisure time. Whatever the occupation at home may be, it is good to have a quiet time before the children go to bed: a chapter of a story, a song or music, and a prayer in bed. Then the children are ready for their nightly journey into the world of sleep and dream. It is not a matter of indifference what sort of content and mood of mind child or adult takes with him into sleep.

It is not only in the course of the day or the year that we are concerned with a process of in- and outbreathing. The whole life of feeling which is so strong in children in these middle years brings them into perpetual sway between sympathy and antipathy, joy and sorrow, hope and fear, those contrasting moods which are nothing other than the in- and outbreathing of the soul. Sorrow brings a process of contraction, both in the soul and in the body: we draw in our breath in sobbing and crying. Laughter expands the soul and empties the lungs in gargantuan ripples that convulse the whole frame and can become an agony if the laugher loses his self-control. In sorrow we look inward and experience our own ego. Many children first realise their own individuality at a time when they believe themselves to have been unjustly treated and go into the garden to nurse their sorrows. In laughter we give up our ego, we are dissolved. The imbecile, who has not achieved the ego, is always grinning. Statues of great antiquity, before the ego was born in the human race, wear the archaic smile. What is true of joy and sorrow is also true of all polarities of emotion. How deeply children love to swing between the poles! What good lovers they are and what good haters! They must always have a favourite colour, a favourite flower, a favourite pudding. What they do not like is horrible and disgusting beyond expression. And how quickly they change. A little girl who has had a bosom friend for a week will make a face when her name is mentioned the week after: but a few days later they are arm in arm again.

For a child in this middle period of childhood life without feeling is almost meaningless. There should be the sway of feeling in every lesson, a time for laughter, a time when the children feel a little sad, sometimes even to the point of tears. How quick they are to feel sympathy with a lonely tree, a dying plant, a hurt animal: how readily they seize on any peculiarity which gives the smallest excuse for laughter. It is a mistake to imagine that childhood can be, or should be, all happiness. In the West happiness is regarded as one of the rights of man. We are entitled to 'life, liberty and the pursuit of happiness'. In the East a different opinion prevails, more akin to the saying of the Buddha that Birth and Life and Death are all suffering. It is not wrong to pursue happiness; but to expect or demand it exclusively is to court disaster. To delight only in the joyful and eschew the tragic is a modern phenomenon even in the West. In his lifetime Dickens was as much admired for his pathos as for his humour, and when he gave readings from his books the audience were shaken by tears no less than by laughter. No humorist of today (except perhaps Charlie Chaplin) attempts the pathetic or believes that he ought to do so. The result is that Western man is often overwhelmed when calamity overtakes him; or he escapes into some superficial distraction from an experience which could immensely deepen and enrich his life. Strength of Soul arises through experiencing both happiness and sorrow, pleasure and pain.

> Joy and woe are woven fine
> A clothing for the soul divine...
> And when this we rightly know
> Through the world we safely go.[1]

[1] Blake.

Naturally, it is not right to bring actual unhappiness to children intentionally, any more than it is right to be dishonest with them and conceal some matter of sorrow in order to keep them happy. But in imagination they have a deep longing to meet joy and sorrow and all the moods of which the soul is capable. It is even a mistake to omit the terrible things which occasionally occur in all stories, including fairy-stories. Fear also is part of life, and children will find a way of inventing fears, however much the adults may try to shield them. The story must accord with the age, but all good stories, like life itself, are compact of diverse moods and emotions.

There is one type of feeling which it is above all important to foster in childhood. Children have naturally an abundant faculty for wonder and reverence. The world is full of marvels, and adults are beings of stupendous capacities and universal knowledge. Unhappily this divine sense of wonder can easily shrink to an admiration of human cleverness as represented by the wisecrack and the gadget. It is all the more important for teachers to consider with great earnestness the mood which the day's lesson will create. There are so many books, so many radio and television hours, so many encyclopaedias and, alas, so many teachers whose aim is to impart knowledge quickly and easily without any element of that faculty which the Greeks said was the beginning of philosophy—Wonder. It is a strange thing that an age which has discovered so many marvels in the universe should be so conspicuously lacking in the sense of wonder.

Yet these very discoveries give abundant opportunity for fostering the faculty of wonder if they are rightly used. To give a single example: in what a matter-of-fact way children are generally told of the law by which all substances expand through heat and contract through cold, with one or two unimportant exceptions such as bismuth and water at a temperature just above freezing. And that is all there is to it. Yet it is on this latter strange reversal of a uniform process that all life on the planet Earth depends. If water continued to contract down to the freezing-point ice would be heavier than water and would sink. The polar seas would long ago have become solid blocks of ice which would have spread and frozen up the Earth. But just before freezing-point the process of contraction is reversed and the water expands. So ice floats, the seas remain unfrozen and life flourishes on the earth. Such facts should be told children in such a way as to awaken in them that quality which used to be called 'awe'. How little of that quality remains with us is shown by the shrinking of Milton's 'aweful' into the 'awful' of modern speech.

It is not merely that a sense of wonder is a good thing in itself. In the alchemy of life one quality is transmuted into another as we grow older. Wonder is transformed into a quality which is rarer today than ever before. It is the beautiful and indefinable quality still possessed by a few older people of creating a mood of graciousness in any society they enter, of conferring blessing on the people they meet, like the blessing of the warm sunlight on a cold spring day. If the lives of such people are examined it will generally be found that as children they were able to look at the world with wonder, and at some grown-up in their circle with reverence. The looking-up with reverence in childhood changes in old age into this inestimable quality of spreading warmth and blessing.

It is a quality much more worth planning and striving for in a school than any immediate intellectual or athletic success. For such an end the first requisite is naturally to find the right teachers, men and women with some richness of mind who are really devoted to their task. But once they are there not a little can be done to help them by the way the school is organised. The continual changing of teachers is inimical to the growth of that kind of personal relationship on which deeper qualities are based. The teacher needs time to understand the child, the child needs time to appreciate the teacher and grows into a proper respect and affection for him. It is therefore a good custom for the Grade teacher in these middle years to travel up the school with his class, if possible until the age of puberty. Not that he will be with the same group of children all day long; but he will always receive them for the first lesson in the morning, and he will be generally responsible for their welfare and progress in the school. Experience has shown that in this way a very intimate relationship is established between teacher and children, fostering that kind of confidence and respect and love which gives stability in middle life and the power of blessing in later years.

There are many other reasons for continuing the Grade teacher with one class over these central seven or eight years, of which a single important one must be mentioned here. This middle period of childhood reflects in miniature the whole process of the child's life in the sphere of feeling, just as the first seven years reflected it in the sphere of will. Until about the age of nine the child demands a preponderance of movement, as he did in the earlier period: he is still compact of will. After the age of twelve a more conscious form of thinking develops. Between these two ages the child lives in the quintessence of feeling and imagination —the heart of the heart of childhood. Even these important changes, however, do not alter the fact that throughout this whole seven-year period the child's thought is fundamentally different from that of the adolescent and the adult. It is unspecialised, it is uncritical, and it is pictorial. We weaken a child's thinking for later years when we make changes in his life which do not take this coherence into account. We strengthen it when, by keeping him with the same teacher, we allow its roots to grow in their proper soil.

It is a great responsibility to teach a group of children most of their subjects for a period of years. It will only be of value if the teacher can waken in himself genuine powers of fantasy and imagination, and present everything to the children pictorially. For this is the way in which children see the world: and in this respect they are repeating the history of mankind. All their early thinking is pictorial: the capacity to think 'abstractly' only properly emerges at puberty. The one is born out of the other.

It has already been said that the first consciousness both of mankind and of the child is a pictorial one. The reason for it constitutes a highly important piece of psychology. We have to recognise that the forming of images rests on quite other powers than does abstract intellectual thought. The latter is an activity which employs the brain. The former is connected with the blood processes which are the vehicle of the will. No doubt this sounds at first very strange. But we can readily discover the active or willing quality in picture-forming even if we consider only the simplest and most obvious form of mental picture, that which we present to ourselves through ordinary perception. When I look at a landscape or a picture or even the face of a friend I am not passively and instantaneously receiving a total impression on my retina, as the film in a camera receives it. I can actually only look at one small portion of the thing I contemplate at a time. My eye travels from one part to another, and the total picture which I present to my mind is the result of my activity in building the parts into a whole in such a way that they cohere together. Thus even the immediate pictures of sense-perception are dependent on an activity of the will. The eye is by nature a very active organ: it searches out the depth as well as the length and breadth of things. And the pictures of sense-perception are created by the activity of the eye quite as much as by its receptivity.

If the pictures of sense-perception are an active creation still more so are those re-creations (sometimes called after-images) which we can summon before our mind immediately after perception: still more are the difficult re-creations of memory: and still more the act of imagination by which we 'body forth the shapes of things unknown'.

Once we realise that the forming of mental pictures is related to the will we understand why all early language is pictorial, why myths and sagas come before science and philosophy, and why the first thinking of childhood is a picture-thinking. It is hard for us as adults to remember how strong was our picture-forming faculty in childhood; with what facility a stain on the wall or the graining in a piece of wood conjured up a house, an animal, or a landscape. It is equally difficult for us to imagine in the distant past of mankind an age when this faculty was so strong that only a few special people could see the world in its unembroidered outlines as we perceive it today.[2]

It is therefore right and proper to present the world to children in the form of pictures because it is natural to their consciousness. But it is important for other reasons as well. It preserves in their thinking the vigour of will which will be so important for them in later life: it enables them to enter with their full life of feeling—that is, *whole-heartedly*—into the experience of thinking: and it keeps their thinking in touch with reality. The last contention will sound strange in an age accustomed to think of reality in terms of physical substance and scientific law. But if you explain such a thing as the formation of rain to a young child scientifically, the laws involved have no meaning for him, and he can only pretend to be thinking about processes which are for him entirely unreal. But if you make a picture of God as the great gardener who wishes to water all the fields and plains and forests of the earth, and takes

[2] The pictures of the constellations are a case in point. Today we see only the separate stars.

the water from the seas as a man takes water from a well, and lets the water fall so gently that it does not harm even the tenderest flower, and is yet so careful of the water that, when all the plants and creatures have drunk, it all runs pure and sweet back into the sea—if you speak in this manner, the child will see the world in terms he can understand, and his thoughts will be real thoughts.

It was because of his great desire to avoid the pictureless abstraction for young children that whenever he himself lectured on education Rudolf Steiner always spoke about the right method of teaching children their letters. For letters in their modern form are 'abstractions' in the sense that the shape of the letter has lost all connection with the sound it represents. In the original picture-writing this was not so. If we were to draw a curling hissing snake every time we wanted to represent the sound 'S', there would be a real connection between the sound and the symbol: and in the case of this particular letter we can see how the picture has been simplified into the simple curved line. That is something that appeals to the fantasy of a child, and if he learns to make the letter 'S' first of all as a snake it will for long afterwards retain something of its pictorial character. If he learns all—or most—of the letters in a similar way, the alphabet will remain alive for him in a manner which is impossible when it is treated as a collection of abstract symbols. By this method the letters are developed from drawing, an art for which children have naturally great love and great capacity. Learning letters from the drawing of pictures presupposes another procedure—that the children learn to write before they learn to read. This is the proper order, because writing calls for greater activity than reading, and the golden rule of education is to go from movement to rest, from the active to the passive, from will to intellect.

It is not necessary to be historically accurate and teach the children the actual pictorial origin of the letters, even if that is known. On the contrary, by exercising his own fantasy the teacher will stimulate the fantasy of the children, who will probably begin to see pictures of their own making in the shapes of the letters as they learn them. But the picture alone is not enough. In teaching each letter the attempt should be made to awaken a feeling for the quality and beauty of the sound it symbolises. Take, for instance, the sound and the letter 'M'. It is the sound which of all the consonants is nearest to a vowel, the sound on which we can actually sing. In order to say it we have to close our lips firmly together: if we watch someone else saying it we notice especially the shape of the mouth. The children should hum many tunes so as to feel the difference between singing on the muted *mmmm* and on the full-throated *Ah*. Then their attention should be called to the beautiful double curve of the mouth and they can be shown pictures in which the painting of the mouth is especially remarkable. They themselves can paint and draw this double curve and gradually develop the form of the 'mouth' into the letter 'M'. Of course they will think of many words in which the sound *m* seems to predominate: the first word that ever opened their lips, Mama —mother: words which express the soft liquid quality of the sound: the hum of insects, the moaning of the wind, the murmur of the waves. It is always good to seize opportunities for teaching them lines of poetry even though they contain long and difficult words (which, contrary to the belief of the compilers of educational Readers, all children love) for the sake of their sound. So by all means let them learn such lines as Tennyson's:

> The moan of doves in immemorial elms
> And murmuring of innumerable bees.

If the children learn to make a letter such as 'M' in this way they learn very much else besides: and what they learn is of the kind that can grow with their growing experience. If later on they come to read Latin poetry they will understand that for the Romans the sound *m* was so liquid, so close to a vowel in character, that a final *m* elided before a word beginning with a vowel, so that *bellum est,* for instance, becomes *bell'est*. When they learn something of India and hear of the sacred word which still resounds from the worshippers in countless Hindu temples, the word AOUM, they will better feel the gradual closing of the lips which the utterance of the word brings about, and with it that sense of inwardness which is a true preparation for prayer and meditation. Should they wonder what St. Paul meant when he said, 'I will tell you a Mystery', they will be led back to the Greek Mysteries, and they will discover that it is the word 'Muo' (meaning 'I keep silence', or 'I close my lips with an *m*') which gave its name to these divine secrets. But now St. Paul is proclaiming abroad what had formerly been wrapped in secrecy in the Mystery

Temples, the mouth is opened, the hidden places are made plain. Thoughts and experiences that can grow as the child grows—these are the life-blood of education. But only a teacher who has shared the experiences of the children in their younger years can awaken them later from the deep places of memory in which they lie asleep.

An imaginative teacher will make the most stony ground grow charming flowers of fantasy, and not a little nourishing food as well. There is hardly anything more arid and conventional and unreal to a child's mind than the complexities of English spelling. Why do we spell the same sounds in such a medley of ways, *bough* and *bow, meat* and *meet* and *mete, pear* and *pair* and *pare*? The wonder is not that many children find spelling difficult but that any of them master it at all. Of course spelling enshrines much interesting history, even historical mistakes.[3] But children have to learn to spell before they can appreciate this—and, truth to tell, the historical approach to spelling has many pitfalls. Nothing is less educational than the practice of learning strings of unrelated spelling words by heart. But sometimes words similarly spelt group themselves in a real picture of life. There is a whole family of words in which the vowels *ea* appear together.[4] 'In the h*ea*vens the sun and moon and stars app*ea*r. The stars gl*ea*m and the sun sends his b*ea*ms down to the *ea*rth, while the w*ea*ther fills the str*ea*ms with water and the str*ea*ms carry it to the s*ea* from where the b*ea*ms of the sun carry it up again to the h*ea*vens. Because of the w*ea*ther and the sunb*ea*ms the *ea*rs of wh*ea*t grow which the farmer r*ea*ps, and the miller makes them into m*ea*l out of which the baker bakes the br*ea*d. When we take our s*ea*ts for a m*ea*l before father or mother d*ea*l out the food we show our gratitude by asking a "grace before m*ea*t".'

Sometimes a group of such words can be formed into a little rhyme:

The sun says, 'I glow',
The wind says, 'I blow',
The stream says, 'I flow',
The tree says, 'I grow',
And man says, 'I know'.

[3] e.g. 'Rhyme', an eighteenth-century mistake for the correct 'rime'.

[4] For what follows I am indebted to a teacher of the Stourbridge Waldorf School in England.

But whether in story or rhyme, something of fantasy and charm, not unmixed with a delicate moral quality, enters the unpromising subject of orthography.

It will be the task of a later chapter to give further examples of fantasy and picture in subjects characteristic of the different ages. It should not be imagined, however, that such things are only for younger children. Right up to puberty (and beyond) children naturally delight in pictures. If any of them learn the Greek alphabet at a later age they rejoice in pictures for the letters just as much as the younger ones with their native alphabet. Any picture or story which enshrines the quality of an age or a place is invaluable to the teacher of geography or history.

The strange thing is that the picture-forming faculty not only leads to the highest aesthetic experience: it is also one of the most practical powers which a man can possess. In life we are always having to face situations which are new to us and perhaps to any man. If we can place ourselves in imagination in such a situation beforehand, if we can *see* in a concrete picture exactly what it will be like, we may save ourselves many mistakes. For we either anticipate by imagination, or learn by the experience of our mistakes. It is better to anticipate by imagination.

CHAPTER IX

Teacher and Child

ONE of the mysteries of the teaching profession is why one teacher is immediately able to keep perfect order in a class while with another the first lesson may go well, the second will be troublesome, and the third will see chaos and pandemonium. You may isolate all the elements necessary for handling children, confidence, friendliness, orderliness, the gift of clear expression, knowing your own mind and so on: but they will all come to nothing unless to them is added the intangible quality of understanding children. It is an art which can generally, though not always, be learnt: but it is highly painful to learn. It means knowing how to adjust yourself in your manner of speaking and behaving to different ages and groups of children. Like all arts, also, it is highly individual, and everyone has to discover his own technique. But the beginning is to understand how very different is the discipline demanded at different ages of childhood.

The right discipline for young children (if so severe a word can be used for them at all) up to the age of the change of teeth is undoubtedly the natural discipline of imitation. Fundamentally small children know what they want to do, and the adult's chief difficulty lies in providing the right opportunities for them to do it. They are never at a loss. But at about the seventh year a new mood sets in. Children become uncertain of their own purposes and look to the adult for guidance. It is a mood which has been charmingly expressed in the following lines:

> Come along in then, little girl,
> Or else stay out!
> But in the open door she stands
> And bites her lips and twists her hands,
> And stares upon me trouble-eyed:
> 'Mother,' she says, 'I can't decide!
> I can't decide.'[1]

It is a curious thing that the 'progressive' school movement of the twentieth century seems almost entirely to have neglected this

[1] Edna St. Vincent Millay, quoted by Gesell in describing the six-year-old.

mood in children. In its reaction against the rigid discipline of former times it stressed only the importance of freedom, forgetting that freedom includes also the freedom to obey. In fact, however, children in the middle years have a deep longing for direction and authority. They respect the teacher who can 'keep them in order': they are uneasy when laxity prevails. It is interesting to see that even when a child has done wrong—and knows that he has done wrong—he tries to find an authority for his action outside himself. Up to the age of ten or eleven, when taxed with his misdemeanour, in nine cases out of ten he will excuse himself by saying another child told him to do it. A Grade teacher who begins with the first Grade has therefore to satisfy this desire in the children for authority in behaviour as well as in knowledge. This is another important reason for keeping the same teacher with a group of children over a number of years. Discipline then arises through the natural acceptance of the authority of one individual. For children a man is a reality: rules are not.

It follows that the teacher must be worthy of the respect which the children so gladly accord to him. This is a formidable responsibility because children have a wonderful belief in human omniscience and omnicompetence. They genuinely believe that you know everything and can do most things. Only very gradually do they acquire any feeling for the hierarchy of social importance. Father or mother may be cook or bottle-washer but in their children's eyes they are as important as an ambassador. Through their confidence in the adult, also, the children have a natural belief in the unity of knowledge. Schools today endeavour in all sorts of ways to overcome the departmentalising of knowledge into its multifarious 'subjects'. But for the children there is naturally no difficulty. It is obvious to them that if the same person teaches geometry and history, mechanics and nature study, poetry and chemistry, knowledge is fundamentally one.

For the teacher it is an exhilarating experience to have to explore so many subjects: and he will almost certainly make the interesting discovery that he by no means teaches those subjects best which he knows best. If he is by training a historian—and has kept some freshness of mind—the excitement of discovering principles unknown to him in magnetism or acoustics will awaken the enthusiasm of the children as well. It is not a question in these middle years of the children acquiring great erudition in a wide range of subjects. An ordinarily competent mind and good will for work will enable a teacher to acquire all the knowledge necessary. It is far more difficult to develop the art of presenting that knowledge to the children in a way that has real meaning and value for them. It will be the task of later chapters to suggest some means to that end. But from the point of view of the coherence of knowledge there is again an enormous advantage in keeping teacher and children together over the years. There need then be no fixed time-table, and the teacher can allow one 'subject' to lead imperceptibly into another: indeed he will do well not to think of his material as 'subjects' at all, but follow the delightful practice of one teacher at a Waldorf School who says to himself as he goes into the class-room each morning: 'I am going to talk with the children about the world.'

At every level, then, reasons can be found for allowing a teacher to go with his children up the grades: and all these reasons lead to the right kind of discipline in building a natural authority between teacher and child. The obvious objection which can be raised to such a practice lies in the personality and ability of the teacher. Are children to be tied to an incompetent teacher, or to one whom they (or some of them) dislike and cannot get on with, for a period of six, seven or eight years? Naturally in choosing a teacher for this task, as for any other, as much care as possible must be taken to see that he is the right person for the job. If he is not, he can perhaps work in some other department of the school. Probably he would be better in another profession. For the qualities which a teacher needs for any teaching of young children—imagination, humour, plasticity—are the ones above all which will enable him to win and retain the respect of children over a number of years. The difficulty will probably be in breaking the bond rather than maintaining it. It is always a moving ceremony in a Waldorf School when a Grade teacher takes leave of his children and gives them over to other hands.

For with the advent of puberty a change inevitably occurs. It is not merely that children now begin to need the kind and scope of knowledge which only a specialist can impart. They approach knowledge and the person who can give it, in a totally different spirit. With their very immature abilities they wish to have their own opinions and make up their own minds. They will not respect an adult merely because he is an adult: but they will immensely respect his abilities and emulate his enthusiasm. The right form of discipline for this age, therefore, is neither imitation nor respect for authority, but comes through enthusiasm for knowledge and for life. The adolescent is critical, often destructively so. We should welcome even this destructive quality as a sign of mental energy. For the teacher's task is to convert this critical propensity into a zeal for the fine distinctions of knowledge, and thus turn destruction into creation. It is a task not unlike that undertaken by the ancient Persians when they converted the wolf, the destroyer of the flocks, into the sheep-dog which preserves them.

It would perhaps be an impossible task were it not for the fact that the secret inward uncertainty of the adolescent makes him long for a hero—of course of his own choosing—on whom to model himself. The whole condition of adolescence, therefore, calls for other qualities in a teacher than those which are sovereign with younger children. As well as being the expert and the enthusiast in his subject, he should be something of a hero to the young people he teaches. It is partly for this reason that teachers in their twenties are often most successful with adolescents, who feel them as leaders walking only a few steps ahead and talking the same language. There is a natural relation between the different ages of life: the small children to the old, the youth to the young man. It may not always be possible to bring such ideal relationships into practice: but it is always possible to remember them and develop the quality of the right age whatever one's actual years may be. It is on the right relation of adult to child that sound discipline must be built.

It is in his conception of the importance of authority and guidance for the middle years of childhood that Rudolf Steiner is most at variance with the 'progressive' educators of today who contend that 'teaching'—in the sense of presenting an organised picture of the world to children or endeavouring to train specific abilities in them—is unnatural; while learning by simple association with adults is natural. A materialist like John Dewey (materialist because he accepts the conventional modern explanation of the origin of life and mind from matter) argues in something of the following way. Education is the handing on of forms of life from one generation to another. In the animal kingdom this is done by instinct or imitation and sometimes by a little very simple teaching. In early primitive societies it was done by instinct and by assimilation from the environment; children picked up the arts of life by mere association with the adults. In civilised societies, however, what children need to know, and the skills they have to acquire, are so complex that they bear no relation to their natural instincts. An artificial world—the school—has therefore to be created for them, in which they are taught these unnatural things. This has to be done: but it can be done in either of two ways: either by direct personal command from the teacher, or by a common understanding of the means and ends of action. The former comes from without, and involves repression and a system of bribes (or rewards) and punishments. The latter comes from within and is emotional and intellectual. Dewey is naturally a strong advocate of the second method, and the whole basis of his 'democratic' approach to education is that the right and natural way of learning is through social activity in which every member fully comprehends the means and the ends.[2]

There are a great many assumptions in all this, most of which have already been challenged in this book. First of all (and very significantly) it is assumed that the purpose of education is comparable among man and animals. Next that civilisation arose out of primitive societies in which life was close to animal life. Thirdly, that obedience to the authority of the adult is unnatural and repressive. Fourthly, that children are capable and desirous of understanding the 'means and ends of action' in a manner comparable to adult understanding. Fifthly, that if a society is to be democratic in the sense of understanding and conducting its own social affairs it should begin with this method of life in the schools.

Behind all these assumptions lurk the fatal legacies of Rousseau and of Darwin, the idea that a civilised state is artificial and a 'primitive' state is natural to man because it is closer to the animal. Nowhere, however, is there a greater difference between man and animal than in the growth of their young—the animal rushing headlong to a fixed and conditioned form of maturity, the child helpless for years in a state of extreme plasticity and adaptiveness. Childhood is a state which has its own changing character and its own changing laws, and at no point is it comparable either to adult or to animal society.

[2] Fair summaries are not easy to make. But the above would seem a reasonably accurate representation of some main contentions in Dewey's *Democracy and Education*.

Moreover, the traditions of mankind are opposed to the view that human societies emerged by social experience from a primitive animal-like state. All ancient civilisations record divine teachers, or heroes, or gods—Dionysus or Osiris or Zarathustra or Numa or Moses or whom you will—who taught them the arts of agriculture or the laws of society by direct inspiration from the spiritual world. Social experience of the right kind and at the right time is of great importance in education. But the historical picture of mankind looking up for divine guidance is repeated in the experience of the child. Only the child looks for the divine in the human adult because he has been shut off from the heavens by the Fall of Man. If he does not find it, he will become a social materialist. The discipline of childhood includes the discipline of reverence for the adult.

* * *

Any discussion of discipline immediately raises the question of punishment, though, strictly speaking, punishment arises, not when there is discipline, but when discipline fails. There are two quite distinct kinds of offences which may have to be visited by what may be called by the common name of punishment: failure to carry out some work or task assigned; and actual unsocial behaviour such as theft, lying or mischievous destruction. As to the first, it is highly important that children shall perform any task which the teacher gives to them. The first consideration, therefore, is that the teacher shall only give them tasks which are in the children's competence and which can be enforced. Homework, for instance, should not be given unless it is certain that it will be done. But if, through the child's fault, a task is not done, it is equally important that he is made to do it as soon as possible. Without this he may lose his respect for the adult which it is so important for him to preserve. To keep a child after school so that he may carry out or finish some neglected legitimate task is not really punishment at all. It is only giving him further educational opportunities.

It is the second kind of offence which calls for real punishment, and it is therefore much harder to deal with. There are, however, two golden maxims to be remembered whenever any question of such punishment arises. The first is that punishment must appeal to the moral sense and must therefore aim at making the child more conscious of what he has done. The second is that punishment is an intensely individual thing, and what would be right for one child would be entirely wrong for another even in the case of identical offences. A choleric child may get into fits of ungovernable temper in which he will break anything which comes to hand. He is quite unconscious of what he is doing at the time, and for him the best plan is to wait for twenty-four hours, then take him to the scene of the outburst and very quietly describe to him, or even act before him, just what he did and said. Punishing him in the ordinary sense of the word would probably make him inwardly angry (for he will feel a certain injustice in being punished for what he cannot really help) and more liable to similar outbursts in the future. A child of a different disposition may commit some act of vandalism out of malice or through sheer joy in destruction. For him it will be important to come consciously to realise the labour which such destruction involves. He may not perhaps be able to make it good himself, though it is best if he can, but he can write and deliver any letters involved, he can make all necessary preparations for the job and clear up afterwards. If in the process he becomes interested in the skill involved, much will have been done to cure him of his destructive bent. It may be he is one of those rare children who seem to feel no sense of shame. In such a case it may even be good to take the child into many classes and raise the other children's indignation against him in class after class. But such a procedure would only be right in rare cases and would do untold harm to a sensitive child. An intimate knowledge of the child is indispensable in determining the right form of punishment for any special offence.

Motive also may be very divergent. For how many reasons will a child steal! In small children it may be nothing more than pure imitation, going to the bag where Mother keeps her money because the child does everything Mother does. Another child may be one of those children who must always be touching and handling everything they see and who generally have dirty fingers and an untidy appearance. Such children are unconcentrated, they live in the objects around them, and the ego-sense is not adequately developed. For this child it is a question of curing his condition rather than actual punishment. To be made to sit every day for ten minutes with his legs crossed, and holding his toes with crossed arms, will be for him at the same time a punishment and a cure. For the crossing even of the axis of vision has much to do with the realisation of the ego; and this is enhanced in the gesture and position described which concentrates the whole body in a kind of double cross. One boy who had been made to sit in this position for a short time every day, after some weeks looked up to his teacher and remarked: 'This is me here and no one else.'

Another child may steal in order to buy something he (or his friends) particularly need. Yet another may be the ugly duckling in the class, and steal in order to be able to distribute largesse of candy or other presents among his fellows and so acquire an ephemeral popularity.

In almost all kinds of offence among younger children, in addition to whatever punishment may be invented, much can be achieved by telling a child stories in which his special failing is characterised. For the child's consciousness is pictorial, and the picture of a story, or the pictures of a dozen stories, will have far more effect on him than any number of scoldings or moral exhortations. With younger children it is not too difficult to make up fairy-tales or fables in which the man who lies or cheats or steals comes to some appropriate bad end, though it must be remembered that the more imaginative the tale the greater will be the effect, and the child should not realise that the tale is being told for his special benefit. But with somewhat older children pictures from real life can be very effective. Take, for instance, an unpopular boy of nine or ten who steals in order to buy sweets and so have the means of making himself popular. His theft is really the responsibility of the whole class who have not been social enough to accept him. So the story has to reprove the boy, but also to condemn the children as a whole and make them mend their ways. It would therefore be good to tell a story in which a ship was sailing on some great adventure but in which one of the crew was extremely unpopular (through no fault of his own) and badly treated by all his shipmates. The ship got badly becalmed and all the sailors, who were great smokers, used up all their tobacco. Now it happened that the unpopular sailor had the task of cleaning the captain's cabin, and this made it possible for him to raid the captain's tobacco-jar. And now all the sailors who had been so unkind before came crowding round begging for tobacco and telling the unpopular sailor what a fine chap he was.

But, alas, the captain came into his cabin one day and caught the culprit in the act. Immediately all hands were piped on deck, the news of what had happened went round, and as they tumbled up the companion-way the sailors discussed what punishment the thief was likely to get. But the captain turned his terrible and righteous wrath not on the unfortunate sailor but on the entire crew. He told them that it was their cruel and horrible behaviour that had driven this man to doing what he did: that every one of them was ten times worse than he was; and that unless they reformed their ways he would not allow them on land at the next port to buy tobacco or anything else.

In a story like this the turn at the end will have a great effect because it will take the children completely by surprise. The unfortunate ugly duckling will experience an immense sense of relief that he has not to carry the burden of guilt as well as of unpopularity. And even the one story may begin to improve the relation between the children.

The test of a good punishment is whether something positive emerges from it. This is perhaps especially the case when a whole group of children are concerned. For a number of children together will do wanton stupidities such as one of them alone would not even have thought of. To use a Greek image, they behave as though the god Pan had entered into them and they had lost their individuality in a common elemental consciousness. It is 'panic' behaviour. The shock of what they have done, when they view it afterwards, will often enable them, if the matter is rightly treated, to make a new step in responsibility. It will probably be best to talk the matter over with the children, or at any rate with the ring-leaders, individually. It may even result in a particularly mischievous child turning his energies in a better direction. The course of life is never all smoothness and harmony, and sometimes social outbreaks, like epidemics, are to be welcomed because they clear the blood and promote a new and healthy growth when they are happily over.

Some of the 'progressive' schools of the present century have adopted the practice of holding courts at which the children themselves judge the offender and assign the punishment. This practice does at least recognise the fact that children expect a certain measure of justice to be awarded, and that the consciences of the children would be outraged if it were not. They still live by the

Old Testament morality of an eye for an eye and a tooth for a tooth. If you are hit you are entitled to hit back: if someone spoils your book you can spoil his. The Christian doctrine of forgiveness is very far from the instincts of young children. This sense of rough justice they have: but to elevate this into judicial capacity and make them little magistrates is not only alien to their capacities, but awakens the critical faculty far too early, and weakens their trust in the adult to whom they instinctively feel such affairs belong.

These are the aberrations of discipline, and the more a school is founded on a true understanding of the changing relation between child and adult the less they will appear. Authority in a school is divided among many people, and it will only become a unity which the children experience if all those people share a common picture of their task and their relation to the children. Sometimes the great artists of the world express profound truths in painting in a far more subtle and telling manner than any words can achieve. There is a picture of the school of Botticelli (if not by Botticelli himself) which might well be taken as meditation for all teachers of children. It is ostensibly a painting of Tobias and the Angel, a very favourite subject among painters of the Italian Renaissance. In the apocryphal Book of Tobit, Tobias is sent by his blind old father on a journey from Nineveh to Rages in Media. He goes to the market place to hire a guide, who proves to be none other than the Archangel Raphael. Raphael is the only Archangel mentioned in the Apocrypha and painters of the story always represent him with young Tobias, who carries the fish he caught in the Tigris and is accompanied by the dog which goes with him on the journey. But in the Botticelli picture there are three Archangels. Behind the boy stands the Archangel Gabriel, holding the lily of the Annunciation, with his eyes turned upward in profound piety to the heavens. Raphael is in the centre of the picture, leading Tobias by the hand: he looks down with loving care on the boy, who looks up to him with unbounded confidence. In front goes the winged Michael, clad in complete armour, with a drawn sword in his right hand and his eyes gazing steadily before him: yet we feel that he is all the time perfectly aware of the boy who follows behind. These are the three archangels of childhood, and the artist has perfectly represented the three attitudes with which the adult should regard the child in his three great stages of development.

An earlier chapter touched on the great mystery of the need of human education and how it came about that children had to learn from human teachers instead of from divine. The contemplation of such a picture as this can help to lift education on to a level at which it may become an inspired task. At that level all the contents of all the books on child psychology seem remote, puny and unprofitable.

CHAPTER X

The First School Years

IN examining the progress of the first seven years a very important principle came to light, the principle by which longer periods of time are reflected in smaller, analogous to the law of 'correspondences' so familiar to former centuries. It has also been mentioned that the same law applies to the second seven years of a child's life, which also fall into three shorter periods of between two and three years, marked by changes of such significance that the British Ministry of Education has made one of them the main turning-point in the whole organisation of the State schools—the celebrated (or notorious) age of 11+.

These changes can be described in a variety of ways. In the first smaller period of the epoch between seven and fourteen much of the principle of imitation still plays into the children's lives. It is remarkable, however, with what fervour they soon begin to reject the idea of 'copying'. There is no stronger term of abuse than when a child of seven or eight points the finger of scorn with the crushing epithet of 'copy-cat'. The children of this age are still very innocent and almost entirely uncritical. The authority of the teacher is quite unquestioned. That is not to say that anyone can keep a class of seven-year-olds in perfect order; only that the children fully expect anyone to do so and are quite helpless when he does not.

From about the tenth year a new period begins. The children notice the teacher more critically. If he is clumsy, if he trips over the mat, or upsets a vase of flowers, or knocks the blackboard over, he will be greeted with laughter in which there is no small element of derision—a thing which would never have happened earlier. It is above all at this time that the children need a link with their own particular teacher, and not with the adult in general. If the teacher is worthy of their regard he can enjoy an unparalleled authority at this age. To the children their teacher is the paragon of all virtues and all accomplishments.

With the twelfth year there is again a definite change. Something of intellectual thought arises in the children's minds as an anticipation of a later stage of development. It is a kind of false dawn which is only too easily mistaken for the real sunrise. Estimates of such things as intellectual ability, whether by examination or by intelligence test, made at this age are only too likely to be erroneous.[1] It is a most unfortunate thing when this change, which is really the crown of a homogeneous period, is made the beginning of a shatteringly new experience in a child's life such as a change of school. For the process by which the picture-consciousness transforms itself during middle period of life into intellectual thought is delicate and gradual. To carry the sensitive, feeling quality which belongs naturally to the former over into the latter is only possible if there is no break in the teaching. To make an abrupt change in the twelfth year is like tearing the muscle from the bone. Indeed this is more than a mere analogy. For from the twelfth year the skeleton plays a part in children's lives which it did not play before. Until now the movement of children is remarkable for its plasticity and freedom. As you watch their graceful easy movements, it is hard to believe that they conceal in their bodies anything so hard and unyielding as a skeleton. They seem to move by blood and muscle alone. But about the twelfth year the character of their movement changes. An awkward lankiness will frequently reveal itself, and it is easy to detect the skeleton in their walk and gestures. This is the outward sign of an inner process. It is not only that definite new developments occur in the skeleton at about the twelfth year—in the humerus and femur, for instance—but that the consciousness which was till now living in the rhythm of blood and breath reaches down into the bones.

In the human body it is only the movement of the bones by the muscles which can properly be said to exhibit a mechanical principle. The bones are levers which the muscles work by means of the sinews. The very development of their bodies now brings the children into contact with something of the mechanical world. With this goes a gradual alteration of their consciousness. A 'bony

[1] Under the British system children are graded into three groups in the twelfth year and sent to three different types of school: Grammar, Secondary Modern and Technical, except for a few 'Comprehensive' schools where the division is internal. There is some provision for redistribution in the fourteenth year but this is difficult to achieve and many Headmasters and Headmistresses complain of a high percentage of wrong grading which becomes apparent as the children grow older.

system' of thoughts and concepts appears in the fluid pictures of their mind. For the first time they begin to grasp the abstract idea. One of the arts of teaching at this age is to find the subjects in which the concrete picture most closely exemplifies the abstract law so that a natural unity is still preserved. Otherwise the new concept is divorced from the older picture—the muscle is torn from the bone.

It is not an easy matter to find the right way of introducing children to the modern world. There is some justification for Dewey's attack on the theory that education should aim at preparing children for their future adult life. He believes that children live in the present, and that an education for the future is always forcing something unnatural upon them. He equally condemns the Herbartian view of the careful selection of content by the teacher as a 'schoolmaster's theory' which slurs over the personal sharing in common experience and denies vital energy seeking for immediate effective exercise.

It is evident, however, that children can only explore a given region of experience at a time. As they are ignorant of the possible fields it can hardly be left to them to choose. The adult, therefore, has the responsibility of deciding what shall be the content of experience. It does not matter whether you believe in the old straightforward lesson, or in the project method, you have the responsibility of choosing the theme. How you treat it when chosen, how much it is made the basis of artistic expression and social experience, is quite another, though equally important matter. And happily there is not necessarily that opposition between the child's enjoyment of the present and the training of a faculty or of a future skill which Dewey seems to suggest. The nature of an art is always in some measure to present the eternal in the guise of the temporal and local; and the art of teaching is to make the enjoyed moment serve the whole of life. Perhaps it is also the art of living.

What do children in their first years at school need to learn and discover about the world? Certainly not the same as the adult. For their attitude to the world is quite different. The adult feels: here am I, and there is the world—the two are separate. But in the first school years the child does not make that division. Everything in the world is endowed with life, feeling and purpose. He says Goodnight to the sun and the trees and the stars as naturally as he kisses his mother. If we tell him the world is what modern man has come to believe, we take the world away from him. He may never get it back.

It is plain that when we introduce him to the world we have to do it in the form of fairy-tales and fables. There everything can talk, there birds and beasts and insects perform works of charity, there metamorphosis and magic reign, and the prince may become a bear and the princess a swan at any moment.

Fairy-tales not only see the world as the child sees it, they contain much of the nature lore, the moral lessons and practical wisdom of our ancestors. It is always sad to see how much is lost when a modern writer puts a fairy-tale into some other form. Walt Disney's *Snow White*—quite apart from any other consideration—spoils the story by mere omission. For in his version the wicked step-mother comes only once to the house of the dwarfs, when she brings Snow White the poisoned apple. But in the real tale she comes three times: first with a pair of stays in which she laces Snow White so tightly that she cannot breathe: then with a poisoned comb: and only thirdly with the apple. In the picture-consciousness of our forebears we have here a representation of the rhythmic man, the head man and the metabolic man. It is in the least conscious part of her being alone that Snow White can be overcome: and she has to experience death—or something very like death—before her Prince can awaken a new consciousness in her.

The older fairy-tales are so important for children just because they are based on an ancient primeval wisdom. Many elements in them can provide the seeds of a more conscious knowledge in later years. In the understanding of different nations, for instance, an important background lies in their folk-tales. How different are the Celtic Irish tales from the Germanic, such as those of the Brothers Grimm! There is a lightness and gaiety, a polished sprightliness about the Irish tales which indicates that Ireland was a country of learning and culture when Germany was still a land of vast forests and tribal simplicity.

It is especially in the first Grade that the fairy-tale should reign supreme. Pretty well all the experience children of this age need can be found in them—pictures for letters, songs, plays, even counting and arithmetic. But the children are descending to earth, and will soon demand a more human element in their stories.

There are two kinds of tales which carry the human character of fairy-stories further, though in different ways. The first is the fable, in which animals not only speak and enjoy human powers as they do in fairy-tales, but personify some particular human quality, virtue or vice. The other is the legend, in which some special person—saint or holy man—lives in such sympathy with nature that he has power over the elements and over the animals. Stories of both these kinds lead the children gradually from the almost archetypal world of fairy-tales to the perception of more human qualities in nature and in man's relation with nature. Fables especially can be culled from all countries of the world. For they are born of a stage of consciousness in which mankind felt (as children feel) that soul qualities were expressed in other kingdoms of nature as well as in man.

As the principal content of the third Grade—which ends the first phase of the central epoch of childhood—Steiner recommended a sequence of the principal stories of the Old Testament. It is not only that you have here the legend at its highest and grandest—Noah with the animals, Elijah with the Ravens, David with his sling and Joshua with his trumpet—but that the whole story is one of the journey of man from Paradise to the earth—that journey which the children themselves are in the act of making. Like the children of Israel they have many things to learn on the way.

Such a development of stories, culminating in the picture of divine guidance of a whole people, is naturally different from anything that would be recommended in a school based on a different view of life. Dewey, for instance, would begin with practical occupations, especially farming, at the age of six, and then gradually expand to all inventions and occupations, and the discovery of the world. He rejects the Herbartian idea of using *Robinson Crusoe* as a picture of human inventiveness, because he finds fiction is unnecessary when the life of Red Indians and the struggles of the early American Colonists up against the forces of nature in the New World are far more real and satisfactory.[2]

The result, however, is the same—to teach children from the beginning that man has always progressed by the exercise of his own cleverness—the sort of scientific humanism which the

[2] Dewey: *The School and the Child.*

twentieth century is gradually overcoming. Children, however, believe in the magical world, a world in which invisible forces directly intervene. A small boy of seven who stoutly refused to believe in the feats of magic performed by a character in a fairy-story was adduced as proof that children of his age had grown out of fairy-tales. But on examination the reason for his disbelief was discovered. The character in question had not got a magic wand.[3] Science fiction is the substitute food of a generation starved of their proper diet of the magical.

Naturally there is nothing to be said against the gradual introduction of children to the observation of the world around them. But it is one thing to do this directly and immediately, and another to draw the observation out of the child's imaginative life. To take a simple illustration, if you want a child to notice the different kinds and shapes of clouds, you can take him out in different weathers and point out the various formations and tell him their names. This will be excellent when he is eleven or twelve. But when he is small you will do better to make up a fairy-tale in which a prince has to go on some journey of high import, and he can only leave when a shining cloud in the shape of a white castle appears at dawn in the sky. He has to wait nine days and see clouds of all shapes and colours and watch how they gather and disperse, before the white-castle-cloud finally appears. Such a story will bring a quality in a child's later observation of clouds which direct instruction cannot do.

The fairy-tale gives a splendid opportunity for the imaginative description of nature. No adult will ever see a mountain as it appears in the coloured photographs of shiny geographical magazines who has read as a child the description of the mountain in George Macdonald's *Princess and Curdie*. His eye will penetrate into the hidden streams and metal veins and dripping vaults: and the light on rocky buttress and wooded ravine will be not the common light of day but that light 'that never was on sea or land'. It is when children have first grasped Nature imaginatively that they should begin to grasp the details of the world around them: if they are in the country, the different kinds of corn and grass and fruit-trees; if in the town (together with as much nature as they can get) the kinds of building material, brick, stone, slate

[3] Gesell notes of the child of seven that he wonders how God works, but thinks he must have a magic wand.

and tile. Few city-dwellers know whether the pavement they tread on is made of natural stone or artificial slabs. But the difference is considerable, and can be felt by the feet of a blind man.

The art of the teacher is to take the right story material and use it educationally. The fairy-tales will give pictures for the letters of the alphabet. The fables will provide little plays in which particular children can act the surly bear or the angry lion or the crafty fox or the timid mouse, and so help to cure themselves of some particular difficulty. Everywhere there will be opportunities for painting and modelling. Perhaps the children will make a calendar of the seasons, every month with its own picture throughout the year. For in painting children have immense courage and will tackle anything. God creating Heaven and Earth is no more difficult to them than a house or a bus.

When they have learnt their letters as pictures—each as an imaginative whole—the first writing exercises will begin. It is a memorable event when a child first writes something complete, like an adult, and the thing written should be something worthy of remembering, perhaps a verse from a poem so simple and yet so profound that he will treasure it to his dying day. The first things children read—and reading naturally comes after writing—should also be beautiful and imaginative, not the banal tales composed to introduce two hundred new words and use each word six times, which are of a stupidity calculated to kill any child's interest in reading for life. For the proper content of education is something that you can carry with you, not something that you leave behind. The poet De la Mare writes in the preface to one of his books that he often learnt as a child things he did not properly understand. Then in later life the flash of enlightenment would come, and he would exclaim: 'So that is the meaning of that!' There are things one can learn as a child which will grow richer in content and meaning throughout the whole of life.

The third Grade marks a definite step in social consciousness, and is a good age for the first practice in simple correspondence. Letters have the great merit that in writing them a child can feel he is talking to someone else—only through another medium. Many children who will talk cheerfully and freely can only bite the ends of their pens when they have to write a letter, as though talking and writing were two quite separate things. The ninth year is not too early to write practical letters also, about some real or imaginary job to a carpenter or a plumber, or about stores to a grocer or ironmonger. The virtue of such practical letters is that the writer has to tell his correspondent all the things he needs to know, and see the transaction through someone else's eyes. It is an important lesson for life, and one which some people never properly learn.

The content with which the child's picture-consciousness should be fed will naturally be different in different parts of the earth and among different traditions of civilisation. Modern civilisation only too readily teaches the same thing everywhere, with the result that it blurs fruitful national distinctions in culture just as it has blurred them in architecture. Every civilisation, however, has its rich heritage of fairy-tale lore on which the teacher can draw.

Naturally, we are not exclusively concerned with the child's pictorial consciousness in these early years. Movement has a most important part to play—and it is the golden rule of a Waldorf School that *movement comes first*. There are many ways of applying it. In learning to write it is good for the children to run the forms of the letters in large size on the floor. Take off their shoes and stockings also, put a pencil between their toes and see if they can write with their feet. All children delight in this experience, and it can be specially good for those who have difficulty in mastering writing. Even in the first Grade in their Eurhythmy lessons[4] the children should walk and run the principal geometrical forms—circles, figures of eight, squares, triangles, pentagons, etc. It is even something of a social education and makes children more aware of each other, if the appropriate number all have to move together in squares or triangles or pentagons without colliding. It is interesting to note that it is frequently the unsocial children who cannot move in time with the others. The dreamy children will probably find it hard to move in sharply defined figures, while the clever little intellectuals may have difficulty with rhythm. An over-intellectualised child will often find it impossible to move in rhythm; he may even be unable to clap or count in time with the movement of his feet. The opportunities for helping children to overcome special difficulties through movement are endless. The difficulties themselves may well have arisen because the children

[4] See the later chapter on Eurhythmy.

did not play out their sense for movement in the earlier years. The place of cure is therefore the place of origin, in the movement system itself.

Allied to movement are acting and speech. It is possible to train children to a high degree of adult perfection in acting, but this should not be the aim. The acting of children should have a quality of naïvety and a breadth of movement which would look ridiculous in the adult. Indeed its charm consists in its perfect innocence. In reciting, also, children tend to exaggerate the rhythm. This does not matter in the least, provided they are speaking the sounds clearly and with feeling—so that you know they are really seeing what the words describe. The poems the children learn to recite should naturally form part of a total experience, perhaps a poem about the season of the year, or one that forms part of a story which is being studied at the time.

It will be noticed that all this involves a certain measure of memory training. For after the change of teeth memory is no longer the fitful visitant which it was before. The child possesses a memory instead of being occasionally possessed by it. Two kinds of memory must be carefully distinguished—the rhythmical and the conceptual. It is the former which is paramount in these earlier years. The child learns his poems, his number tables and so on by a rhythmical process. But he will also retell a story in his own words, through remembering the sequence of pictures, and in this he approaches conceptual memory. It is here especially that the greatest care should be taken not to overtax the memory, but to exercise it in the right way. Memory is akin to the process of sleeping and waking: a particular memory wakens in us in the same way as we ourselves wake from the dim consciousness of sleep. It should therefore be brought into relation with the rhythms of sleeping and waking. It is not good to call on memory without an interval for sleep. Ask the children to retell a story after a night has elapsed, and it will be most interesting to observe which of them repeat it accurately and perhaps somewhat prosaically, which enrich it by some development of their own, and which are merely confused, or perhaps alter some main feature of the story to suit their own situation. This last will often prove the case with a story told to help a child in some special difficulty, whose will-consciousness may reject the very suggestion which would help him. For instance a very timid child, who would never play with the other children, was told a story of a baby sea-gull who was afraid of flying down from his nest high up on the cliffs to join the other little sea-gulls in catching fish. At last a kind uncle sea-gull came and took the little sea-gull on his back and flew with him down to the sea. Once he was in the water he found he could catch fish just as well as any of the other young gulls. When asked to repeat this tale the following day, the timid child stopped at the point where the uncle sea-gull took the little one on his back. Pressed to continue, she finally added: 'And the little sea-gull fell off and was drowned.' So deeply do even children resist the medicine that would do them good.

The retelling of stories is a highly important educational process. But it should not stop at retelling. Allow another night to pass after the retelling, and then, by questions or some other means, awaken the children's thought about the story. Why did this or that happen? Would it have been better if some difficulty had not occurred? By such a treatment of the story you will on the one hand guard against over-straining the memory, and, on the other, you will encourage memory to become creative and fruitful. To put it in another way, you will be making a healthy connection between the sleeping and waking elements in the soul.

We have so far been speaking mainly of stories, in which the possibility of appealing to the picture-consciousness is obvious. It may well be asked what can be done in the beginnings of such a subject as arithmetic in which there is strictly only pure thought. For a child, arithmetic is naturally first of all concerned with the counting of actual things, or at any rate of imagined things, rather than with pure number. And in this fundamental approach there is not a little room for fantasy. If they are using real objects for counting let them be things of beauty which it is a pleasure to handle or which have some imaginative suggestion—nuts or acorns or flowers or eggs. Precious stones would also be very delightful! But in these first simple number sums there is one very important consideration. It will make a great difference to the tendency of his thinking for the rest of his life whether you fill the child's mind with the idea that one and one and one make three, or whether you start with three and break it into its parts. Ultimately and logically the first leads to the idea that the universe is composed of atoms. The second, the grasping of the whole before the parts, is the way of imagination, and leads to the view that it is only the whole which gives meaning and existence to the parts. The difference is as subtle as it is profound.

Starting with the whole makes it possible also to introduce another gesture into arithmetic. Addition, the adding of unit to unit, always contains something of the suggestion that the object is to get more and more. Subtraction leads readily to the picture of giving away to others. So, if it is to be a gardener with a bunch of roses he has grown, let him be thinking: if he has twenty roses and gives a beautiful bunch of six to his neighbour and seven to his wife, how many will there be left over for his friend's little girl who is very ill in bed? Or if it is a mother squirrel taking her nuts from her store to the nest, she must be pondering—tail in air—how many she will need if each of her little ones is to have five. The children should only know that they are learning about numbers. Actually they are learning something of far greater importance—a moral attitude to life. Naturally the time will soon come for straightforward sums, but it is the quality of the first approach which is of vital importance.

It is important also for another reason. Many children become frightened of mathematics for the rest of their lives because the introduction was too complicated or seemed to lead to a world of absolute rigidity and fixation from which there could be no escape—a nightmare world. Starting with the whole—sum or product—gives a possibility of variety which is a real relief to certain children, and encourages a more mobile way of thinking in all. Five and three can only make eight: four times three can only make twelve. But eight can be the sum of five and three, or four and four, or six and two: twelve can be the product of both four and three and six and two. You are not caught in the only possible answer.

It is equally important to approach arithmetic from the quite different point of view of rhythm. All children love counting. Who has not lain in bed as a child and set himself the quite impossible task of counting up to a thousand? When children are learning their tables the more there is of rhythmic movement—chanting, clapping, walking, stamping—the better they will learn. It is the only way in which many children will remember them at all. For quite a number of years some children will have to say a table through rhythmically before they can tell you what is eight times nine or seven times six. There is a beautiful phrase used of music by Elizabethan writers, 'making division'. It is a wonderful thing to bring the experience of singing into a child's feeling for number, and it will be good for them all to learn the names of the notes. While some are singing one long note, others can be dividing it into two, four, six and so on. If the children have learnt to play recorders or flageolets (as they all should) the playing of the notes while they walk in time, each to his particular 'division' is an excellent mathematical exercise. For it means that the children experience number with every part of their being.

With the end of this first phase of school life the children are naturally more conscious, more observant, more on the earth than they were at the beginning. They are ready for a new outlook on life, and it is right to prepare their minds for the next stage. For this some elementary grammar will be helpful. For it is in grammar that we first realise distinctions within thought itself. The children should at least know the difference between nouns and verbs and adjectives—though it is a pity that in English these terms are so colourless and forbidding. Here is the opportunity to use in another domain the lessons in simple practical life which also eminently belong to this age.

For all children should know the principal operations in such fundamental skills as farming and house-building. To make some real butter by stirring cream (and chanting one of the old 'butter songs') or to mix some real lime-mortar and watch it hissing and bubbling are things of the greatest value to children. But it should be an ideal picture which they are given. In farming, it is the loving care of the farmer for animals and crops and soil which should be brought to the fore, together with the wonderful inter-dependence of plant and animal: in house-building, the need for all the different trades to work together so that carpenter and brick-layer and tiler and plumber all give their skill at the right time and all know exactly what has to be done.

All this gives a splendid chance for the practice of grammar especially if the teacher remembers the golden rule that movement comes first. For of course the start will be made with the verbs. What does the farmer do in spring, or summer, or autumn, or winter? Can you come and act some of the things so that the other children can guess what they are? Who will show us all the things a carpenter does? Or a plumber? All these names for what all these people do we call *verbs*. And how many tools does a farmer or a carpenter use? Can you draw them? All their names are *nouns*. If he is a good carpenter and keeps his tools well, what will they look like? If he is a bad one and neglects them, what will they be like then? All these words are *adjectives*.

There is a month's work in a single paragraph. And the children are not only learning the elements of grammar, they are bringing to life in a new way something they have already absorbed. It is a real and concrete exercise in thinking, and opens the door to 'fresh woods and pastures new'.

The mention of a month's work will fittingly introduce a practice of Waldorf Schools which is of great importance to the Class Teacher. As it is the aim to introduce new thoughts and new material to children when their minds are fresh in the morning the Class Teacher (as also specialist teachers in the High School) always has his class for the first lesson in the day—a lesson which lasts up to two hours. If he is to make every lesson an experience for head, heart and hand he will need this generous measure of time. During this Main Lesson (as it is called) he will teach one subject for several weeks and so bring the greatest concentration upon it. Naturally the ratio of learning to activity, of listening to speaking, of receiving to giving, will vary with different ages, with different subjects and with different seasons and days. A skilful teacher will soon learn to notice whether his children are becoming tired. He will know whether it is through too much imagination, or too much reasoning, or too much variety, or too much monotony, and will act accordingly. If the subject of the lessons has been especially imaginative, full of stories and pictures, he will find the opportunity of introducing some mathematical work. If the children weary of arithmetic he will find some relevant story to give them relief.

Within the framework of a general plan for the year the Class Teacher will decide how long to pursue one subject and when to pass to the next. There will be constant opportunities for recalling in one subject things learnt in another, but it should not be the ideal for a child to remember as much as possible of what he learns. It is only when knowledge sinks into deeper layers of the soul that it becomes capacity. Even in such elementary things as learning to ride a bicycle we achieve the skill by forgetting the process. Those public figures who from time to time inveigh against the waste of their school-days, because they remember so little of what they were taught, are unaware of how much they owe to what they have forgotten.

CHAPTER XI

From Nine to Twelve

THERE are two main reasons why the tenth year is of quite exceptional importance in a child's life. The first has already been described. It is that he is approaching the very centre of his childhood, in which the formative powers, working from the head downwards, are meeting the forces of 'awakeness', rising up from the limbs. The other is that an event is occurring which corresponds to the time when a child first uses the word 'I' in the initial period of his life. At that time—about the third year—he first reveals a certain egotism (if it may be so called) in his actions. Seven years later, in the tenth year, he shows a distinct enhancement of this ego-sense in his life of feeling. It is this which also enables him to devote himself more consciously to his teacher or to his parent—if he finds in them the qualities he needs.

It is interesting to see the characteristics which an observer such as Gesell discovers in this tenth year. He described self-motivation as its cardinal characteristic. For the first time a child can interrupt a task and return to it purposefully, and he likes to perfect his skill by repetition. His conscience develops and he wants to be straight. He has elementary ideas of justice and can accept blame. In the sphere of knowledge he becomes interested in the distinctions between different flags, types of cars and so on. He also likes clubs with passwords, codes, tabus—and such clubs are generally confined to one sex. In fact he is an individual and we should tolerate his idiosyncracies.

All this is very true. It is only a pity that Gesell should think that this 'deepening of emotional life . . . is, of course, due to underlying growth changes in the physiology of his neuro-humeral system'.[1] The growth changes are there. But they are the lever by which the child lifts himself to new experiences, not the cause of them.

These changes have to be rightly met in the process of education, and it is good that attention should be drawn to them. For changes of this kind have a fundamental meaning and importance

[1] *The Child from Five to Ten.*

compared with which differences in intellectual ability are superficial. Yet in most schools it is intellectual ability which determines the grade into which a child is put. Who ever heard of a child being promoted because he was exceptionally good at painting or music, or because he excelled at acting or needlework? It is just this intellectual ability, however, which masks the deeper processes of life on which a true education will be built, irrespective of the variety of intellectual attainment. Naturally this variety also must be reckoned with, but not as the fundamental issue. In a Waldorf School the children are kept together by age in order that their educational experience may meet the deepest needs of each stage of life. A certain period in history, a certain science, a certain process in mathematics should be taught in conformity with the child's needs. What he can do with it will depend in part on his intellectual and in part on his artistic or imaginative ability. The theme is given by the age, the variations by the ability and temperament.

The tenth year will serve as a good illustration of this principle. At this age wide varieties in intellectual ability are already apparent. Some children will read almost perfectly while others still struggle with all but the simplest words. Some can do sums running into thousands, while others still jib at the tens. But behind this lies the same profound psychological change stirring in the depths. It is this which it is the prime task of education to meet.

How is this to be done? A whole book could be written on the tenth year alone and it is only possible here to give some characteristic indications. But they must be enough to illustrate at least one attitude which it is essential to maintain. It is the attitude of relating all things to Man. There is nothing new in this. From the Greeks with their proverb that 'Man is the measure of all things', to Goethe who believed that 'the whole world reaches in man its own consciousness', it was taken for granted that in some way all nature realised itself in Man. The new thing is to speak about nature as unrelated to Man—except for purposes of utility or, at best, by sharing similar accidents of evolution. We saw the unity of the human and the natural world in fairy-tale and fable. The children now need a new connection with nature, but much depends on whether the human centre for which they instinctively long can be preserved. If it can, they will continue in their later life to regard the world as their home in a way which is given to few people in the modern age.

At this age, then, Man will be the centre from which we shall start our exploring and to which we shall always return. Let us suppose that we are investigating the animal kingdom—and it happens that the fourth Grade is an excellent time to do so. We shall not begin by going to the Zoo to see wild animals in confinement, however good the conditions may be. We shall start by talking with the children about animals they know, in such a way as to form an imaginative picture in which the animals are seen in relation to man.

We can begin with the human head. The children will describe it as round, and perhaps they will remember how they used to draw it with a circle and big teeth in the mouth. It is hard outside, to protect the soft substance of the brain within. It has many windows to let the outside world in, and these windows open and shut in different ways. The eyes have actual shutters, but we can also shut our ears, though they have no shutters, and sometimes we do so even when something very special is being said to us. The air comes in and out of the double doors of our nose: and the mouth is a very remarkable door because we open it to put our food in, but in return words come out of it. If the food is good we are healthy; if bad, we become ill. But if our words are good they make other people healthy; and if they are bad they make other people ill. So we have to be even more careful what comes out of our mouth than what goes in.

The head also does not like to move very much; if we wag him about for long he gets dizzy. He likes the world to come to him rather than for him to go to the world. In fact he can be very lazy unless we make him work. Are there any animals which are hard outside like the head, and even try to be round like him? Yes, the shell-fish that lie under the sea all day. They are lazy too. And they open their shells to let the sea wash in their food just as we let the light wash in at our eyes, and sound at our ears and air at our nostrils. Even those that have only one shell like the limpets loose their hold on the rocks to let the water wash through them. In fact they generally hold on very lightly and if you manage to take them by surprise you can get them off quite easily. But once you have woken them up they hold on terribly hard. There is one animal like a shell-fish without a shell; and he doesn't hold on to the rocks. If we draw a man's head and imagine that, when we look at something, two arms really come out of our eyes to take hold of it, and when we hear something another two out of our ears, and when we smell something another two out of our nostrils, and when we eat something—well our jaws are just like two arms ready to take hold of our food; if we draw these eight arms coming out of the head (they are there really, but we don't see them) then we have—the octopus. So the octopus is like a head that can move about without either body or legs.

Our trunk is very different in shape from our head. It can bend and twist this way and that because, instead of being covered with a hard shell, it has beautiful ribs, like the ribs the waves make in the sand when the tide goes out. Are there any animals that are all body and ribs just as the octopus is all head? Surely the fish, with their wonderful flexible skeleton. They dart and twist this way and that, and jump out of the water without any legs to jump with, simply by coiling their bodies up like a spring. But what a tiny little head the fish has! No wonder he lets himself get caught on a hook.

Our legs again are quite different from either head or body. In fact they are just the opposite of the head because their bones are inside them, not outside as in the head. A great many animals have legs but they are really all land animals. And their legs are all sorts of different shapes according to what they need to do with them. What fine legs a horse has! But do you see that the joint in his back legs, where you would expect the knee to be, bends the opposite way to a knee? Why is this? Yes, it is because this joint is not a knee at all—it is the horse's heel! The horse with his hind legs is always standing on his toes, just as you do when you are going to start a race. He is always ready for a race!

Compared with a horse's legs a cow's seem very thin and weak—almost like sticks. She, too, is standing on her toes so we can see that once upon a time she had to run too. But then she got so many stomachs that she couldn't run any more, and it is quite enough if her legs can hold her great body up, while she chews and chews and chews.

Then have you noticed the legs of a mouse? His hind legs are longer than his front, so that he can jump both high and quickly. But you will notice one great difference between all these animals and man. They have no arms! Even a monkey has not really any arms; for he does the same thing with his legs and his arms, he climbs trees and swings from one branch to another. He has really four legs, and these legs do for him what the legs of all animals do—they help him to get his food, they are just the servants of his body. But the arms of a man are quite different from his legs. And why is that? Because a man stands upright, and so his arms are freed from the earth. What wonderful things he can do with his hands and wise fingers! But nothing is more wonderful than when he does something for a friend or neighbour. Then he is least like an animal: then he does something that no animal can properly do. Then he is really a man.

There are many other ways in which a start can be made from a vivid picture of man to explore the kingdom of the animals. We can remember the age-old tradition of the sphinx, which united the hind-quarters of a bull with the forelegs and chest of a lion, was clothed with the wings of an eagle, and bore the head of a man. All the creatures again united in man! For what is the part of the cow which is most developed? The digestive process. Fancy having more than one stomach and digesting your food twice over! No wonder the cow has such a ponderous body. But look at the body of a lion. What a mighty chest he has surmounted by the glory of his mane. But when he turns round and we see his back parts, how very slender and even feeble they look. What lungs he must have to make that mighty roar! When he goes hunting all the other animals stand still and tremble when they hear him. His eye is quite red because the blood pours in such a mighty stream from his heart over all his body. All the animals fear him but he fears nothing. That is why we say that a very brave man is 'lion-hearted' such as the famous English king who went to the Crusades and was called 'Cœur de Lion'. But if the lion is the King of the Animals, there is also a King of the Birds. He lives high up in the mountains and with his huge wings—very much longer than your arms—he can fly right above the mountain peaks till he looks like a little speck. You know what bird this is—the eagle, and you have probably often thought you would like to be able to have wings with which you can fly as high as he can. But you really have those wings. They are your thoughts with which you can voyage through the seas of space right up to the stars; and perhaps one day you will even be able (as some men have done) to reach the heaven where God and his angels are. For your thoughts fly quite as swiftly as birds. When the great poet Homer, of whom you will hear a great deal one day, wanted to describe something moving very quickly he said it was 'like a bird's wing or a thought'. Perhaps if we could see your thoughts they would look like feathers, and some of you would have very beautiful wings with lovely colours, and some would only have very little wings with dull brown feathers. But, unlike the birds, we can change our feathers and even if they are rather small now we can have wonderful plumage when we become men. So it is no wonder that the sphinx had the head of a man: because a man can have the strength of a bull and the courage of a lion and the swiftness of an eagle.

If in some such way as this—it is only a bare indication—you show the children the animals grouped round man, you are again helping them to see with the imaginative-eye at the same time as they learn to look with the sense-eye. And on another level from the fables and fairy-tales, the animals become teachers of a morality which is born out of the very physical structure of man. Such a view of the animals will also help the children to understand better in their later years many of the old religious traditions. It is not for nothing that the four Gospels were always connected in the history of Christianity with the four beings of the sphinx, the bull with Luke, the lion with Mark, the eagle with John and Matthew with man.

To most children the animal kingdom is of greater immediate interest than the world of plants. It is certainly more obviously related to man; and if man is our starting-point, it is not too much to let the interest in animals dominate the whole of a year before advancing to the world of plants. One of the arts of education should be a lively anticipation. It is good for children to feel that next year something new and wonderful is going to come to them. The worst thing is to be in a hurry.

It is not so easy to make man our starting-point in approaching the plants. It is only later on that the children will fully appreciate the fact that the structure of the plant is actually the reverse of the structure of man. For the plant too consists of three systems—root, leaf and flower. But it is the lowest part of the plant, the root, where the mineral forces are active, which corresponds to the mineral nature in the human head. It is in the flower that something like digestion takes place, some flowers even devouring insects, while the breathing process takes place in the central system of the leaf, as it does in the central system of man. Indeed the breathing of the plant and the breathing of man are complementary to each other—perhaps the largest and most striking example of symbiosis.

All this involves ideas which the children will only be able to follow up in their later botany lessons. But even in the eleventh year they can see pictorially what will later be developed into scientific concepts. From what they have already learnt about man they will know that warmth is not evenly distributed over the body. Our heads are cold—and if they get hot, as they do in a fever, than we cease to be able to think. Our digestive organs are hot—as hot as you were when you had measles—and if they were as cold as the head we would never be able to digest our food. It is only in the rhythmical part that we are 'just right'—neither too hot nor too cold.

If you think about it, you will realise that you have never held a complete plant in your hand! Because a plant is quite different in the different seasons, and you cannot hold all the seasons of the year together in your hand. In the cold of winter the plant's life is in the root—and indeed the root continues to live in a kind of winter in the cool dark earth all through the year. Then comes the light of spring and charms the leaves from ground or stalk. Even in the hot days of summer the leaves are always listening for the breezes to come and keep them cool and temperate. But the flower—out of which the fruit is born—delights in the hot sun of midsummer. It does not want to live on to the autumn when the world will be cool again. So the flower tries to grow up to the sun, and when it finds it cannot reach the sun, it dies rather than live on to the autumn. But if you were turned into a plant and were put in the earth you would have to stand on your head. For that is the cold part of you, like the root of the plant. And all your digestive organs are the hot part, which would like to grow up to the sun like the flower. So you are really a plant with the root in the air: and the plant is you with its head in the ground. And a man should always have all the seasons in him like the plant. When there is something to be done he should be all warmth and energy—he should even try to reach the sun. But when there is a knotty problem to be solved, he should be as cool as can be in his thoughts, and really get to the roots of things.

From such a beginning you can begin to find out which plants principally develop the root, which the leaf and which the flower. It will also give the different stages of plant growth more meaning to a child if plants at different stages are compared in a simple way to the development of his own mind, and it will afford an opportunity to make him a little more aware both of how far he has already travelled and how far he has still to go. When he was very little he slept all day away from the light like the fungi in the woods: then he began to develop a little but he was still very tender like the mosses. Then he began to be a little bolder, to call himself 'I' and open his eyes more to the world like the ferns and gymnospores. Then he began to have all sorts of wishes and thoughts which he never had when he was younger and he became like the fully mature plants with all their different parts. But some of the plants are much simpler than others: some have leaves with only parallel veins while those of others form a wonderful pattern: some flowers have not even got proper petals while others have a cup or calyx of green sepals which holds a corolla of beautifully coloured petals. Perhaps you have only reached the stage of the simplest flowers as yet, but you will soon have both calyx and corolla. Such a way of talking about plants meets the growing desire for fine distinctions; but the classification still has a human flavour. We do not forget man when we look at the beauty of the plant.

One additional point is worth noticing before we leave the plant. As they pass the tenth year children begin to be interested in causes of phenomena, not the conscious purposes by which they accounted for everything before. It is far better that they should meet the idea of causality for the first time not through mechanical concepts but in connection with life. The form and nature of a plant in the arctic regions or up a high mountain is a response to the conditions prevailing there, and must be quite different from the form and nature of a plant in the temperate regions or the tropics. This may be called a 'living' cause, and will not lead to the mechanical world picture which has really sprung from the fact that man has come to associate causes too exclusively with mechanical operations. Here also education should endeavour to guard against the one-sidedness of the age.

The progression from man through the animals to the plants will naturally lead to the mineral world. But the study of the minerals should not arise until after the twelfth year when the mineral part of man—the skeleton—begins to play the part in the child's life which has already been described. In such a sequence we are again following the golden rule of beginning with life and movement, and ending with the lifeless and immobile. It is the way of childhood and the way of creation. Before progressing to this stage, however, there are other aspects of these central years to consider.

There is no time when children will grow well if they are starved of stories. By the tenth year they are ready to leave the simpler world of fairy-tales and encounter the broader and more historical pictures of mythology. It is remarkable how much the mythologies of various peoples differ from each other in mood and emphasis. The Finnish 'Kalevala', the Norse Sagas and the Greek Myths are like paintings in different media and tones. It will be good if in the course of their school-life children hear many mythologies, but naturally in different countries tales will have paramount importance. In the European tradition the old Germanic sagas were completely overwhelmed at the Renaissance by the myths of the Greek and Romans. Sculpture, Painting and Literature drew their major inspiration from these Mediterranean tales and a knowledge of them is essential for even an elementary appreciation of European culture. But at the end of the nineteenth century the Norse myths were again resurrected and have had a profound influence on art and literature, not to mention the Celtic Tales of Ireland which underwent a parallel revival. It is a good thing to find some sequence in the tales which are chosen, something which connects them with the development of the child at a particular age. If we consider only two—perhaps the most important two—of the various mythologies, the Norse and the Greek, it is evident that the Greek is more conscious than the Norse. The Greek Gods sit about debating with each other, and each of them knows very well what he is doing and why he is doing it—nor are the reasons always commendable. But there is no character in Norse mythology to correspond with Athene in the Greek. Loki has a kind of instinctive cunning which is quite different from the serene wisdom of Pallas Athene. But there is a gigantic vigour in the Norse tales which the Greeks cannot emulate. They have no Thor who throws his hammer away and always receives it back into his hand again. It is for this reason that the Norse mythology—or one which has the same quality—is more suitable for children in the tenth year than the Greek. They find in the Norse characters a splendid expression for their new sense of vigorous individuality. Any teacher can discover this for himself if he makes a play for children of this age out of Norse legends. They will love to act Thor and Loki, the Giants and Baldur and Father Odin 'one-eyed and seeming ancient'. The Greek myths—historically the prelude to consciousness—should come a little later, preferably in the eleventh year when they form a fitting introduction to the first historical lessons. For it was the Greeks who created the art of history as they created so many other things. Before them there had been chronicles of a king or of a people, but nothing of that sense of the interaction of diverse forces and wills, or of the development of a process in time, which is the essence of historical study.

Perhaps no subject has been taught to children more haphazardly or with less regard to their development than history. Actually it is only during the central part of this middle epoch of childhood that children begin to develop any real sense of time. Before that, as a natural sequence to the legends of the former year, they will love to hear biographies of suitable famous men. The story of great deeds meets and stimulates their new sense of the individual will. But they will have very little feeling of period: 'once upon a time' is still sufficient for Alfred the Great or Marco Polo or Abraham Lincoln. But by the eleventh year this is changing. The rhythmic system is yielding its forces to consciousness and history is needed to strengthen the newly won sense of time.

Where should we begin? Some educators, like Sir Richard Livingstone, have argued that history is meaningless for children because they have no sense of affairs, and cannot have, until they encounter the experience of life.[2] This, however, is to deny imagination. Shakespeare did not need to commit a murder in order to experience the state of mind of a murderer. No doubt the imagination of children will only lead them into some aspects of history. But even this is a great deal. Not to introduce children to

[2] *The Future in Education.*

history on the grounds that they have got to partake in it first, is as though you were to decline to tell them about another country till they had been there.

It is because we are still building on the child's imagination that it is not the best thing to make the start with contemporary or recent history—but rather with those periods in which history is born out of myth and legend. In the case of the Greeks the Trojan War is half legendary and half historical. Such a character as Odysseus repeats himself, with all his cunning and resource, in Themistocles. Thersites is re-embodied in Cleon. The war with Persia has the quality of a battle between a David and a Goliath. But out of all this is born logic and science and politics, to say nothing of an achitecture and an art which has adorned the world. In fact the Greeks historically made that transition from picture-consciousness to intellect which is taking place in the children themselves. But the intellect of the Greeks still worked with and on the living forces of the world. Their mind hardly reached the mineral world and they considered that thought was a matter of the heart rather than of the brain. There are therefore quite exceptional reasons for introducing the children to Greek History just at this time of the eleventh year. But Greek History and thought are much more deeply rooted than used to be supposed in the history of the East. The children should therefore know first of all some of the stories of Egypt and Persia and India, even if in a very simple way. It will give an opportunity of reviving the Bible stories from another point of view. And when Alexander carries Greek thought and culture to Egypt and Persia and India the children will know to what sort of lands he is going.

The historical approach to the world must be balanced by a growing understanding of the life of their own time and place, if all the needs of the children are to be met. They have already learnt something about the work of man which they see immediately around them, house-building, farming and the like. By the eleventh year they should hear about local industries further afield. What sort of cultivation is there in the country around them and why: what raw materials are found and what use is made of them. The actual chemical processes in industry will come later: but the relation of man's work to the earth is something which it is important for the children to grasp.

It is not the intention of this book to lay down a complete

curriculum even if that were possible or desirable, but to show by illustrations how certain kinds of subjects meet and strengthen a child's development at different ages. In this sense we have spoken of the kind of picture of nature and of men that is suitable for this central period of all childhood. But something must be added about the less pictorial subject of arithmetic.

In arithmetic there are two methods of approach, the practical and the purely mathematical. All sums to do with practical life should be as real as possible. If it is a question of costs, the prices should be those which are actually being charged in the neighbourhood and not fictitious ones. It is good also if sometimes different children contribute different items to a common task. Perhaps the cost of a house can be worked out, in which one child finds the cost of the bricks, another of the flooring, another of the nails or pipes, others of different kinds of labour. This will give the opportunity of reviving on a new level of thought all the children learnt about house-building in the more innocent days when the thought of cost hardly entered their minds. The different assignments will be given to the children according to their ability, but all will contribute to the common task. If some house is being built in the neighbourhood, and its actual cost can be worked out, so much the better. Many social questions will be opened up: labour hours, comparative pay, insurance, workmen's compensation and so on, of which children should now begin to be aware.

From the point of view of pure mathematics, however, nothing is better than for children at this age to encounter fractions and decimals, which provide a further opportunity in a different field for the principle of going from the whole to the part. To grasp the idea in fractions that the bigger the number in the denominator the smaller is the fraction; or, in decimals, that if you go to the left of the point the numbers get a bigger and bigger value, but if you go to the right the value becomes smaller and smaller—this is an exercise in thinking in which children can experience something of the symmetry and formal beauty of mathematics. For in mathematics, as in all other subjects, you will have a profound and beneficial influence on children if you bring their sense of the beautiful into the heart of all that they learn. Artistic children—often little inclined to mathematical studies—will show great interest if they discover that there is beauty also in this subject.

The mention of the artistic element leads to one final consideration. Throughout this middle epoch of childhood painting and modelling should never be divorced from ordinary lessons and relegated to a specialist teacher. For that is a way of teaching children that art is one thing and life is another. But if subjects are taught artistically there will come times when the absolute need will arise to paint or model, as part of the process of learning. Even in mathematics the experience of symmetry or contrast can be expressed in drawing or painting. In a world of specialisation and disintegration it is the task of education to keep a child whole (or sane) as long as may be. And if the teacher cannot paint himself? Then he must endeavour to recapture the ability which his own education destroyed. If he tries to do so earnestly and strenuously he will stimulate and inspire the children to paint better pictures than perhaps he will ever paint himself. He must follow Churchill's advice to those who have never tried to paint: 'Have a go.'

CHAPTER XII

The Twelfth Year and After

ENOUGH has been said about the change in children during the twelfth year to indicate the sort of development which should now take place in the curriculum. The forces of growth are now reaching towards the limbs, while the power of 'awakeness' is mounting towards the head. There is therefore a real anticipation of puberty at this time: the limbs begin to grow a little lanky and the mind a little critical. Adults such as Lewis Carroll, who find small girls so charming, discover that their favourite Alice is leaving her wonderland at this age—and look round for a successor.

It is now right to begin to introduce the first ideas of modern science, and during these three years all children—boys and girls alike—should acquire at least an elementary grasp of the great scientific discoveries of the modern age and of the principal inventions on which modern Western life depends. But once again the method of beginning is of supreme importance, and will make all the difference to a child's whole relationship to science. The first science lessons should be observational rather than theoretical. Far too many children know all the theories, but cannot tell you what they could see with their own eyes, if they had been encouraged to use them. They will know all about the solar system and perhaps about spectro-analysis of the stars, but they cannot tell you the state of the moon or point out the constellations. They know theories of evolution, but not the names of the trees or plants around them.

It is a particularly happy thing if the first sciences can also be related to the child's artistic experience, so that the artist in him is not left outside when he enters the temple of science as is commonly the case in the modern age. For this reason such a subject as simple acoustics makes an excellent entry into the world of science. Not only can children make a great many observations about how sound travels—and they will be astonished to discover that it travels better through water and solid matter than through the air—but they can discover some of the wonderful principles, which meant so much in Greek thought, underlying the phenomena of the stretched string. To sound the note of a stretched string, and then discover that to obtain the octave above the string must be divided exactly into half, is a great joy to children. They realise that the ear is a mathematician, perhaps a better mathematician than they are in their conscious heads. They can make little 'riders' to sit on the string while it vibrates and work their way to the 'notes'. They can discover the numerical proportions of all the musical intervals and, if the string has a pulley at one end and weights to attach, the relation between the note and the tension. Perhaps they will also make pipes of bamboo as a practical culmination to the period. They will certainly look with more interest and understanding at the register of the organ in church with its 16-, 8- and 4-foot closed and open pipes and its 'mixtures' of two or three ranks.

It is better not to have elaborate apparatus. It is good when the children make it for themselves. But for some demonstrations the best apparatus is advisable. For instance, the formative power of sound, which is revealed by the patterns on Chladni's plate, will only show to advantage on a sensitive apparatus. The patterns are of such great beauty that they should be seen at their best.

The phenomena of colour provide an equally good opportunity for observation, in which artistic sense is the ally of scientific inquiry. Here again the right beginning is not with theory but with what the children can see. If they look intensely at a patch of green and then turn away they will see a patch of red; if they look at red they will see green. The laws of complementary colours can be approached from such simple observations: then the question of primary and secondary colours, and how the secondary colours are formed by the actual mixture of pigments or by the meeting of beams of coloured light. The appearance of colour in nature and such interesting peculiarities as coloured shadows can be studied. The children are too young to learn the mathematical theories of Newton, but they should certainly observe the way in which colours are produced by a prism. If their observation is accurate, they will notice that a prism does not break white light into the spectrum as most people are taught, but that it only does so when the light is bounded by a darker object. It was this fact which the poet-scientist Goethe especially noticed, and which led him to form a theory of colour, very similar to that of Aristotle, in which colours are seen as arising through the conflict of light and darkness. When we look at what is dark through a medium filled with light we see the colour blue, as when we see the sky or a distant range of mountains. But when we look at a bright object through a darker medium we see it as red or orange, as when we see the sun through the smoky atmosphere of a city, or look at the electric light through a piece of semi-transparent paper. The children need not be troubled at this age with the controversy which arose between Goethe and the Newtonian school—perhaps they were talking about different things. But there is no doubt that for the artist (who is allergic to mathematical vibrations) and for the naïve observer the Goethean approach to colour is of great interest and value. It is certainly most stimulating to children.

In this first scientific year it is better to introduce a number of sciences from the observational point of view rather than pursue one or two further into theory, which can be done in the following years. We are concerned here principally with the introduction of various kinds of subjects; their continuance from year to year either alone or in their connection with other subjects must be taken for granted. To add other examples, Heat is a subject which readily lends itself to observation and simple experiment. The fact that practically all substances expand through heat can be illustrated in many ways—railway lines, thermometers, steam-engines—already known to the children in their daily life, as well as by many experiments. The different ways in which various substances burn should be noticed, nor should the part played by Fire in religion and mythology be forgotten. Some elements of electricity and magnetism should be introduced both because they form so important a part of modern life and because the whole earth is called into play in their activity. The lines of a magnetic field which can be shown through iron filings are a beautiful and exciting example of making the invisible visible. Indeed, the difficulty in such observational science is to know where to stop.

All these early scientific lessons give admirable opportunities for exercising the art of accurate description. Few people can describe in an accurate and orderly manner some familiar object like an apple or an orange. It is an important art to learn.

The same development which makes such observational sciences a proper study for children about the twelfth year means that they are also ripe for some understanding of the mineral kingdom.

Here again the method should be that of going from the whole to the part. To bring a fragment of granite or limestone into a class and talk about its chemical composition is to detach it from the earth. First of all the children should form an imaginative picture of chalk hills, or limestone ridges, or granite mountains—and if they live in one such district all the more should the teacher help them to see it with the imaginative eye. What happens to the rain when it falls on these various soils, what kind of trees and flowers grow best on them, what crops they produce and, above all, of what they are formed and how they got there—to deal with these questions is to keep the mineral world in its true connection with the living earth. It makes a profound impression on children to know that the great chalk and limestone and marble masses of the earth are the creation of living organisms. If they learn this at the right age their minds will not be closed to the idea that it is the dead which comes from the living, and not the living from the dead.

This introduction to science should go hand in hand with a suitable advance in mathematics, especially in geometry. It has already been mentioned that the foundation of geometry should be in walking and running the principal geometrical forms as a social exercise in the Eurhythmy lessons. The same principle of beginning with movement should be followed in introducing geometry in the form it should now take. If you draw a triangle in white chalk on a blackboard it is quite static and lifeless. But if you take a piece of white elastic and pin it at the two ends along a horizontal line, you can pull it up or down by the middle to form a triangle which can freely move. Then you can make the apex move vertically so that a succession of isosceles triangles appears: or you can move it round in a circle until the triangle disappears into a straight line and then suddenly appears again under the horizontal line instead of above it. Many other figures can be treated in the same way. It is good also to call the children's attention to all the places where they can see geometrical forms in movement—shadows that change during the day, the light of a turning head-lamp on a wall, the curve of a skipping-rope and the beautiful set of a sail.

Practically all children love to make geometrical drawings. Who was not delighted when he first discovered how to draw a six-petalled flower in a circle and practised the art assiduously on the fly-leaves of all his school-books, as the monks of Cistercian monasteries practised it on the plaster of their walls? Children will delight to draw sequences of figures in movement and will invent many new ways of making patterns by following some geometrical principle which will give them instruction as well as pleasure. They will also see that when the apex of a triangle is brought nearer and nearer to the base line, the angles at the corners grow smaller as the angle at the apex grows larger. Then the corner angles disappear just at the moment when the apex angle becomes a straight line—two right angles. But the sum of the angles is plainly the same—they always make two right angles. Thus the children perceive an important law of geometry through movement before they learn the logical proof.

Such geometry of movement can be developed into something of great interest and value. Imagine a triangle of which every point of each side is advancing at an even pace towards its central point. Each of the straight lines will become slightly curved, and if we halt the movement soon after it begins, the shape the triangle has now reached will resemble an ivy-leaf. But, if the movement continues, the middle point of each side will arrive at the centre before the other points. Then as each line passes through the centre a new form will arise, no longer a leaf but a three-petalled flower. We see a metamorphosis taking place by geometrical law: and by taking regular figures and bringing them into movement according to similar laws—though sometimes more complicated—we can produce the principal forms of the plant world. Through such things the saying of Plato that 'God geometrises' becomes concrete and real. It is always good when children discover that what they can create through the inner world of thought is also manifested in the outer world of nature. There is a beautiful saying of Kepler's about his discoveries of the laws of planetary movements: 'I think God's thoughts after him.' Something of that mood can be brought into the first lessons of geometry—a harmony of the outer and inner worlds.

There is the practical side of mathematics as well as the ideal, and with their widening interest in affairs around them it is now suitable to introduce children to some of the simpler commercial practices. Conspicuous among these is the question of loan and interest. As long as they think concretely children do not understand the idea of interest at all. It is obvious that if you borrow a spade, what you have to return is a spade—not a spade and a trowel. Children have much sympathy with the medieval idea that it is wrong for money to bear interest because you make 'a breed of barren metal', and only the living can breed, not the inanimate. Interest sums are therefore important at this age because they are a help to the children to develop the more abstract kind of thinking to which they have to attain. But such practical arithmetic should be closely related to what is really going on in the world around them. Nothing can be more abstract and arid than problems about unknown people investing unreal sums in imaginary undertakings.

To conclude the sketch of this important twelfth year, it chimes well with their general development if children now hear about the Romans and the Roman Empire. For in Rome men began to stand on the earth as they never stood before, and purely human personality asserted itself for the first time. But it was in this epoch of history, when Palestine provided the meeting-place of the Greek understanding of the *Logos*, the Roman gift for Law, and the Jewish feeling for Destiny, that Christ was born. Indeed, almost in the moment when the official Roman doctrine claimed that in the emperor a man had become a god, the Christians held the opposite belief that God had become Man. One of the most obscure periods of history is that in which the Christian belief transforms the Roman belief, or—to express it in political terms—the Roman Empire becomes the Holy Roman Empire. But for the Western people, at any rate, it is the central process in history and it is most important to avoid implanting in children's minds the only too prevalent idea that there is Ancient History and Modern History with a vacuum called the Dark Ages in between. The fact is that, if ever there was a unified period of history, it is that in which the tradition of Rome unified the whole of Europe, the tradition of Greek and Jew civilised it, and the growth of Christianity ennobled it. Naturally children will only grasp this in elementary pictures. But only by grasping it will they understand later what it meant to Western Europe to make a breach with Rome, a fearful and fateful adventure, like leaving the security of home for a voyage without chart or compass on unknown seas. What happened to man in that voyage (which was indeed a physical as well as a spiritual one) is something for the following year. For here again the good habit can be observed of stimulating anticipation and, in the manner of the old novels issued in fortnightly parts, breaking off just as the hero has been swept in a little boat to sea or left alone in the jungle.

When children have passed their twelfth year they are well set towards the greater change of puberty. During this time they are discovering both the world around them and the world within them in a new way. It is small wonder that many questions arise in them which they hardly know how to formulate and probably would not wish to put to an adult even if they could. It is therefore especially at this age that the experience of life and knowledge brought to them should be such as to meet and answer their hidden questions. It helps them greatly also if the same teacher, in whom they have for so long placed their confidence, can stay with them through these years. It is not necessary that they shall come to him with their troubles, though they may well do so. He represents something stable in a fluctuating world and the fact that he is in the background gives the kind of security which a small child in bed feels in the knowledge that his parents are downstairs.

If we consider again first of all the subject of Nature Study, we have seen how in previous years these lessons began with Man and progressed through the kingdoms of life down to the mineral, all in a pictorial and moral way. But children have now a new interest in the physical body. They need detailed physiology lessons. They should learn about digestion and blood circulation and respiration and the function of the nervous system. It is good to deal quite extensively with hygiene at this age when the body is still to some extent an object among other objects and the children are in no danger of becoming worried about their health. The mechanical part of the body, the skeleton, should also awaken the children's admiration. Small children find it hard to believe that there is a skeleton inside their own or anyone else's body. One small child, taken to a museum and shown a skeleton, was told that everyone had one inside him; he looked at his parents with a wondering eye and said: 'Daddy may have one, but not you, Mummy.' But by now the children need to know about the skeleton, precisely because they are realising the forces of it in their own lives. A mood of religious awe can be awakened at the wonders in the structure of the human body.

It is in connection with learning about the bodily functions that some reference to sex finds its proper place. This question is not as easy of solution as many psychologists and educators suppose, who think that it is solved by simple frankness from the earliest childhood. Chidren have no difficulty—especially if a baby is born while they are young—in understanding that a child's body grows in its mother's womb. But the connection between procreation and human passions which is a result of the Fall of Man—this is something which can be very shocking to a sensitive child when it first comes to have meaning for him at puberty. There is something also of which modern psychology takes no account—the quality of Innocence. There are spheres of the soul in which Innocence is a potent force, and if a child has the gift (as some children do) of going through puberty in a state of innocence it may mean much for him in later life. It is therefore a matter of great tact to find the right way to speak of this matter.

It is best to begin with the broadest possible considerations by speaking of the part played by universal forces in the development of every seed. The mere fructification of a plant seed will do nothing unless there are the right conditions of moisture, air, light and warmth surrounding it. Even with these the seed only provides the opportunity for the formative powers of the universe to take hold of matter and mould it into form. It is the same in all other kingdoms of nature. The male seed has its part but it is only a small and momentary one. A new organism is always created through universal forces.

More will be said on this subject in a later chapter on puberty. But it is by such an approach in the pre-puberty age that we create a balance by which the children may be saved from becoming obsessed by sex, as, to a large extent, the whole world is obsessed at the present day. One result of this obsession is the common belief, stemming from some modern psychology, that in such practices as masturbation, or in a natural interest in what later become the sexual organs, children are already enjoying sexual experience in their earliest years. Such things bear about as much relation to the puberty experience as banging the keys of a piano with a chubby fist bears to the art of music.

Inevitably, as they become older, children begin to feel the breaking up of knowledge into specialised departments. It is therefore especially good at this age to introduce comprehensive and pictorial ideas, such as the idea of polarity, in which many branches of knowledge meet. The Grade teacher has to realise that the unity of knowledge which he has so long represented in his person will disappear when he leaves his children. He will therefore endeavour to awaken in them a way of thinking which will prove a key to open many doors. He should never lose sight of the fact that the ultimate unity of knowledge is in man: and by returning again and again from every subject to this common centre, he will establish the foundation of it in later life.

For instance, as a complement to their knowledge of the human body, children should learn about the structure of such organic substances as starch, sugar, protein and fat, and their importance in nourishment, while at the same time the distribution of foodstuffs over the earth should be studied. The staple foodstuff of the East—rice—is the polar opposite in form and manner of growth to the Indian corn which belongs to the West. The former has its fruit dispersed on a multitude of tiny stems: the tight cob of the latter grows out of the stem close to the ground. Thus we see in the staple food of East and West the polarity of expansion and contraction which belongs both to the peoples and the regions of the earth which they inhabit: the Eastern people (until they caught the Western fever) so open to religious experiences, so little concerned with the earth; Western man so concentrated on his task of working the forces of the earth, with so little time or care for meditation: the former smoking the opium which drives man out of himself into a state of delicious dream: the latter dependent on the tobacco which steadies the nerves and helps him to be a collected personality.

It is the same contrast which we see in the great continental peninsulas of the Southern Hemisphere: the hard contracted bony shape into which South America tapers: the scattered islands of the East Indies and the Pacific. But where there are polarities there is also a middle term. So the typical grain of Europe is wheat, whose ear is neither formed of branching spikelets like the rice nor gathered to a cob like Indian corn. The great African peninsula is similarly the mediator between South America and the Pacific islands, neither scattered like the one nor contracted like the other. Indeed, this polarity of land formation between East and West is to be seen in a number of places. In the Mediterranean the Western peninsula of Spain is one solid mass of land. The Greek peninsula breaks into a thousand scattered islets.

Italy, with its few large islands, holds the balance between the two.

Puberty is the time when children may be said to have reached the earth—and reached it in the country and age in which they are born. It is therefore natural that in the last two years of this middle epoch of childhood the history lessons should bring them to the modern age by dealing first with the age of the great discoveries, and then with that of the Industrial Revolution. The interweaving of the new theories of the heavenly bodies with the new laws of physics that takes places between Copernicus and Newton, the rejection of the old authorities in knowledge and religion, the enlargement of man and of the earth, a Shakespeare creating a new picture of man while a Hakluyt delineates the earth, old worlds appearing out of the past while new ones beckon mankind to fresh adventures—all this is matter enough for the historical study of a year. At no time does the world present more exciting personalities engaged in more wonderful and varied adventures. Tycho Brahe, Galileo, Leonardo, Cortes, Drake and a dozen others, all of them filled with that spirit of adventure and inquiry which is dawning in the children at this age, and which may turn to gangsterdom if it does not find its right activity and its proper heroes.

It is only too easy for Western children to feel that civilisation began in the modern age—or even later—and that everything before was unbelievably primitive. It is therefore important that they shall realise that almost invariably a gain in one direction means a loss in another. The age and the countries which saw the birth of technical inventions had little time and less gift for the arts. There were no more cathedrals or stately churches after the Tudors. England, once the most musical nation in Europe, was busy with power-loom and steam-engine while Germany was producing a Mozart and a Beethoven.

It is not only the scientific and industrial side of history which children can appreciate in these last two years with their Grade teacher. They can enter into the great political divisions of the age, such as that between the monarchical and the republican ideal. The ideas that lay behind the American War of Independence and the French Revolution, or the earlier English Civil War, ideals which come to expression in such great characters as Washington, Franklin, Lafayette, Cromwell—these would have had little meaning for them before this age, but they can now arouse their enthusiastic interest. The social conditions resulting from the economic revolution will awaken the children's moral sense. Generally, social and cultural history provide a background to political and economic. For children it is better the other way round.

To keep pace with all this there must be a corresponding advance in mathematics and science. In mathematics it is natural that the year that brings the children Galileo should also bring them the laws of motion and the principles of mechanics. The wheel, the pulley and the lever should all be known. It is good to get some tackle and let the children pull each other up. A miniature set of pulleys merely demonstrates to the eye. A builder's rope-and-tackle speaks to the muscles and the bones. In the sphere of pure mathematics should come the first introduction to algebra. The idea that instead of writing $15=6+6+3$ you can write $x=2y+z$ takes the mind further into the process of abstraction, but also into a world where many wonders are waiting. Children who, for some reason, have found arithmetic troublesome may discover that they can make a new start in algebra—and their confidence in arithmetic is restored. Geometry also is carried further. The beautiful Pythagorean theorem, for instance, should be understood in several different proofs. In geometry man enters a world where thought is self-supporting and self-sufficient. It should beget an immense confidence in the power of thought itself, a confidence which has suffered a sad decline in the modern age, when the simplest proposition has to be supported by statistics, and the habit of appealing immediately to the sense of truth, which was still strong as late as the time of Emerson, has been almost forgotten. A book which ventures to do so will today certainly be criticised as 'unscientific'.

Not much has been said about the teaching of English during this middle epoch of childhood. The fact is that the practice of good language in speaking, listening and writing should form part of every lesson. It is good to make a habit of reading aloud passages from the best authors in connection with any subject under study. The learning of poems should be a regular practice. By the time they reach puberty children should have a small anthology by heart, and by no means only those poems that they can entirely understand. There is a tremendous difference between children in their capacity and liking for reading books. But it is good to encourage them assiduously to read books in connection with what they are principally studying. There are many books of mythology and folk-lore, many simple biographies, many descriptions of different countries very suitable for accompanying the development of studies which has been described. Books, however, which are either childish or aim at giving quick information—such as encyclopaedias—should be avoided.

To illustrate their history, children should now begin to read historical novels. It is probably almost useless forcing those children to read who show no inclination to do so. They will be all the less likely to read when they are older. But practically all children immensely enjoy being read to. We should remember that reading silently to oneself is a comparatively modern practice. A Roman author gave readings of his works, or a slave read aloud to his master. Perhaps it was then even impossible to read silently. It is recorded that when St. Ambrose read the Scriptures people were amazed that he did not even move his lips. We should not then be too surprised that many children do not easily take to silent reading. But teachers can encourage children by reading passages of novels aloud; and if parents would revive the excellent habit of reading aloud in the evenings they would create a bond with their children far greater than the sharing of television can ever bring.

Drama now begins to have special significance for children. Of course they have taken the greatest delight in acting almost since they could speak, and they love to see a play even though it is far above their heads. But drama in the sense of the clash and contrast of character with character, this it is important for them to experience as they come towards puberty. The more external of Shakespeare's plays will now present them with a series of characters admirably suited to their stage of development—Hotspur, Glendower, Falstaff, Prince Hal and many others. But it is a great pity to introduce them to the profounder plays before they are mature enough to appreciate them. Perhaps some things should even be kept for manhood. It is a mistake for children to think that they can know and appreciate everything.

A final word with regard to grammar. It is not good to give too much formal grammar in a child's native tongue. Formal elements are better studied in a foreign language, especially in a logical language such as Latin, if it is learned. The important thing is that the language he speaks shall help a child to *discover himself*. As the inner life develops more strongly with the approach of puberty two faculties take on a new intensity. On the one hand a child develops stronger inward desires. He begins to have his own secret wishes for his future life as well as those openly expressed for holidays, presents and so forth. On the other hand, the world, as he learns more of it, can awaken in him a still stronger sense of wonder and reverence—or even intense surprise. Here we have a polarity. In wishes, the direction is from the inner life to the world: in surprise, the world strikes into the inner life: in wonder there is a balance between what we receive and what we give.

Up to this time most of what children have written will have been of a factual and descriptive character. But it is now an excellent training for them to appreciate and express those moods of soul in which there is an interplay between Universe and Man, in wish or wonder or surprise. The wonder of Cortes when he first saw the Pacific, as Keats describes it in his sonnet, the wish of David that he had died for his son—'Would God that I had died for thee, Absalom, my son'—these the children can emulate from their own imaginative experience, and so win a new appreciation of the perpetual giving and receiving between man and the world around him. In the age when children are finding so many new things in the world, language then becomes the handmaid and interpreter of experience.

CHAPTER XIII

Foreign Languages

WHEN a child is small a more than natural instinct guides him to select those things in the outer world for his imitation which he needs for his inner development. He learns the three essential human activities: to walk, to speak and to think. Without the influence of his environment he might struggle to his feet but he would have no words to awaken his thoughts: without the inner impulse and capacity, environment would produce no result. There is a perfect mutual relationship at this time between the inner and the outer worlds.

It should be the aim of education to maintain, however imperfectly, that harmonious relationship: to teach nothing to a child *merely* because he will need to know it in later life, or because it is thought he will need to know it, or because his parents knew it before him: but only to teach him what—in manner and matter—meets and helps the process of his development. Conversely, to teach a child *merely* for present use or enjoyment is to occupy or entertain him, but not to educate him. What he rightly and enjoyably does now should prepare him for what he will rightly and enjoyably do in the future. The child is a child but he is so *sub specie hominis*.

All this is no doubt a counsel of more than human perfection: but the preceding chapters have shown that it is at all events possible to begin to think along these lines. If the attempt is made to follow it, some things will be learnt earlier and some later than is generally the case, while most things will be learnt in a different way and with a different emphasis. But in the end, children will be better equipped for life than by other forms of education. For they will know as much of the world, and probably more, and their inner powers will reach maturity undamaged.

Among the subjects which have not been touched in the foregoing sketch for a curriculum is one of the highest educational value—the teaching of foreign languages. What foreign languages should be learnt will naturally depend on many circumstances: that the learning of at least one enlarges the mind and trains the power of thought is incontrovertible. Even if no opportunity comes for foreign travel, to realise how differently one nation thinks from another through the very forms of its language is a liberating experience. Two languages are not beyond the capacity of most children, and it is good if they are of a different nature such as German and one of the Romance languages, French or Spanish or Italian.

It has already been mentioned that language teaching can well begin in the Nursery Class, when the vocal organs are still malleable and the power of imitation unimpaired. It is naturally better that the lessons from the beginning should be entirely in the foreign tongue, but all absolute rules are to be avoided. The same kind of direct teaching through songs and rhymes and little plays can be continued at least as late as the ninth year without any grammar or writing. In itself this gives excellent opportunities for combining learning with activity and bringing a strong element of will into the growing life of thought. Indeed, languages provide an unrivalled field for the exercise of the rhythmical powers and for the practice of the golden rule of movement first.

But there is also the happy fact that children remain a little younger in foreign languages, and will be content to continue with fairy-tale plays and fables later than in their own tongue. When children have suffered from a deficiency of these things, the language lesson can be used for something like a process of re-education. A lost childhood can in part be recovered in the nursery rhymes and songs and tales of a foreign land. In the copying of speech-sounds the power of imitation is revived: the will is strengthened by action and the constant repetition needed for remembering.

From the tenth year, writing and reading in the foreign tongue can begin in a very simple way. For instance, the children can write—and illustrate—a fable or a poem they have learned. With this comes some simple grammar—a useful corollary to the grammar they are beginning in their own tongue. It is now, when their rhythmical memory is so strong, that the children can begin to recite or chant such things as tenses and declensions and parts of verbs. The more this is associated with rhythmical clapping and stamping and walking, the better it will be both for the child and for his knowledge of the language. If any translation is done it should be the aim to give the general meaning rather than construe word for word. The more the children speak themselves and the more they learn by heart, the more they will develop the habit of thinking in the foreign language and not translating into it.

Especially in foreign languages it is important that children should have opportunities of showing each other their recent work in poetry, singing and plays. In a Waldorf School this is provided for by the habit of having regular Festivals or Assemblies at which all Grades show to the whole school, and to the parents, anything they have been doing in singing, music, eurhythmy, gymnastics, drama, languages and so on. The last play a very large part in these assemblies. The little children look up with awe to the difficult plays performed by the seniors: the older children are reminded of the foundation of their knowledge in fairy-tale and fable and singing game.

From the twelfth year a new advance is made consonant with the new powers of thought which develop at this age. It is now good to introduce folk-lore and descriptions of the people and country. Such descriptions can be linked to geography: but an account of France in the French language and in the French manner is entirely different from one in a more phlegmatic tongue. The children should now be able to retell a simple story and make small compositions in the foreign tongue. They can learn something about its leading writers, act a few scenes from a play, and compare the form and metre of its poetry with that of their own language. How different is the French alexandrine from English blank verse! How perfectly a French classical play is formed compared with the looseness of Elizabethan drama. The precision of French speech can prepare children for a proper understanding of such contrasts at a later date.

The learning of a language requires rhythmical repetition if it is to sink into the sphere of custom and habit—the sphere of the life-body—to which speech properly belongs. For subjects which have a specific intellectual or imaginative content a period of rest, or even forgetfulness, is advisable. We embark on a subject like chemistry or geography or history with all the more zeal if we have had an intermission from it. For this reason such subjects are taught in a Waldorf School in the period lessons already described: but languages follow a regular weekly rhythm.

Acquiring a skill is not the same process as acquiring insight and enlarging the content of the mind.

More will be said on the subject of languages in the High School in later chapters. But we must not forget here the modern revolution in practically abandoning classical languages in favour of modern. It was by no means Steiner's intention to exclude the classics from the curriculum of a Waldorf School, even if, under pressure of other work and in modern conditions, it has proved in practice difficult to do them justice.

The classical languages present their own peculiar problem. There is nothing new in the discovery that they can be taught in a more living way than by the grind of grammar with which they have often been associated. The Renaissance schoolmasters discovered the talent children have for acting, and Latin plays abounded in the schools of the sixteenth century. Indeed, the schoolmasters were partly responsible for the interest in drama and the supply of child actors (especially for female parts) without which there would have been no Globe Theatre and no Shakespeare. But in the sixteenth and seventeenth centuries Latin was still a living international language. Scholars conversed in it: foreign despatches were written in it: and works of science such as Galileo's writings on Motion and Newton's *Principia* passed immediately into general currency because they were in Latin. But this measure of life has now been taken away from it. It is nonsense to treat a dead language as though it were alive, and unreal to believe that modern children can learn a highly inflected speech in the same way as they learn a modern uninflected tongue.

What are the reasons for learning a classical language at all? The highest, no doubt, is to enjoy the greatest literature the human genius has produced, and to encounter Western philosophy, poetry and science at its source and origin. Alas, in how few of those who have spent years at school and university in the study of the classics is this ambition realised! How many of them in later life prove either capable or desirous of taking down a Latin or Greek book for an evening's relaxation or instruction? Nevertheless it will be a great loss to Western civilisation if contact with the classics is broken. Those children—they are not hard to recognise—who have a natural gift and liking for classical languages should receive every encouragement to pursue them. But have the classics any place in the lives of the less gifted?

It is a great pity for anyone to be completely detached from a whole field of human culture, and especially from one which has had so tremendous an influence on the history of the West as the classics. If it is good for every child to learn some of the principles of mathematics, even though he may never use them in later life, it is not less good to make some contact with the classical languages. When only one ancient language can be learnt there are many reasons for following the usual custom of making this Latin. Predominant among these are the facts that Latin was so long the central language of Christendom, and that only through knowing Latin is it possible to recapture the concrete picture which lies behind the multitude of abstract Latin words which we use every day. It is notable, however, that the pattern of Latin teaching—inherited from the Renaissance—generally entirely omits the Christian and medieval Latin in which the language was most deeply charged with human feeling. Children, however, are nearer to medieval Latin than to classical, just because it is the feeling quality which they understand. Their minds are more akin to the Hymns of Prudentius than to the Odes of Horace.

The Latin of the Church also evokes a direct experience of a most important age of history. You will get the flavour of early Roman Christianity more effectively by learning that magnificent early Christian hymn *Dies Irae* than by a lot of historical study. It is possible to teach the elements of Latin as a historical and religious experience rather than as the training in logical and exact thinking which is generally considered to be its virtue. That training must be made good in other ways: but this new object makes it both sensible and important to include Latin in the usual curriculum of a school. Whose life will not be enriched if he can remember from his childhood some of the songs of St. Francis in the language in which he wrote them, or repeat the *Te Deum Laudamus*, that magnificent expression of the faith and hope and wisdom of a tremendous age?

When all has been said in favour of Latin, however, and especially of this new attitude towards it, the fact remains that Greek is a far more exciting and imaginative language than Latin and has much more in its literature that appeals to children. When the two were commonly learnt together they made an admirable balance to each other. But it is the Latin quality which has dominated the world: it is the Greek quality which the world most lacks. For Latin is the language of fact and reason: Greek of imagination and idea. Nor must we forget that the New Testament was written in Greek as the *lingua franca* of the Mediterranean at the time. From Greek sources came the understanding—and the words—for the sublime teaching of the Creative Word which was with God and was God. It can be a deep experience for a child if he learns in Greek the opening verses of the Gospel of St. John and can write them down in Greek letters. It might make not a little difference to the thinking of the world if all those children who today learn Latin learnt Greek instead.

However that may be, there should be time in the curriculum from the fifth or sixth Grade for some elements of Latin or Greek, or both, taught in an imaginative way. Children who have learnt their own alphabet as mere conventional signs will delight in learning the Greek letters as pictures. Even for those children who cannot pursue the study, something of Greece and Rome will reach them through the sounds of the language in a way which translations cannot emulate. They will have heard the echo of another manifestation of the Word which was in the beginning.

During this time it will easily be possible to discover the children who have a native gift for the classics and who (if they are to continue) should begin a more systematic study of the necessary elements. Especially in the sphere of grammar there is for these children much rhythmical learning by heart to be done which is natural to the middle years of childhood but becomes irksome at a later age. If this is provided for, there will be only gain in postponing to a somewhat later age much of what is commonly taught too young. There is no subject in which more time has been wasted by too early an approach than the classical languages.

CHAPTER XIV

Practical Work

MANY reasons have been given for the practice of allowing the Grade Teacher to take his children up the school, if possible, as far as the eighth Grade. His fundamental task is to unfold a picture of the world and use it for the children's active experience and for the development of their life in feeling and in thought. For this, the Main lesson, with its concentration on one subject at a time and its intervening periods for forgetfulness, is the best medium.

There are some subjects, however, which call for rhythmical repetition rather than periods of hibernation. Among these, languages have already been specially mentioned. But practical activities also—handwork, woodwork, gardening and so on—require their own measure of regularity even if it is conditioned by seasons and availability of rooms and teachers, especially as the children grow older.

It may or may not be the case that the Grade Teacher will be able to take one or more of these subjects. It would be a remarkable man who could take them all, so remarkable that, if he could do so, it would be highly beneficial for the children to be with him all day. Probably, however, a number of teachers will be needed for these lessons, and, if this is so, some account should be taken of whether the Grade Teacher is a man or a woman in arranging them. For the Grade Teacher may naturally be of either sex. It is a mistake to imagine that unless boys have a man teacher they will become uncontrolled. When discipline depends ultimately on physical force this may be the case. But when it springs from long personal connection and from respect for knowledge and capacity a woman often proves a better disciplinarian to an unruly class than a man. The intermingling of men and women teachers is anyhow a natural corollary to the co-education of children.

In arranging its lessons the aim of a Waldorf School is that each day shall become something like a picture of man. If we conceive the first lesson—the Main lesson—as primarily devoted to *thinking* (though a thinking permeated with feeling and will), then the rhythmical subjects will follow after a necessary break: and, last thing in the morning or in the afternoon, will come practical activities or games which exercise the limbs. Head, heart and limbs will then find their right sequence in the day. If the children wish to continue some school task at home in the evening, they should by all means be encouraged to do so, but regular homework can well be postponed until the twelfth year. Even then every effort should be made to see that it is of an artistic character. Nothing is worse than for children to go to bed with their minds wearied and worried by intellectual problems. If possible, also, homework should have an individual character, or at least be in accordance with the child's temperament. It is both more interesting and more social if the children bring divers work to school which contributes to some common whole, and not a uniform task which is corrected to see who has got it right.

There should naturally be a close co-operation between the Grade Teacher and those who take such specialised subjects as practical activities. These should not be organised independently for their own sake but in connection with the curriculum as a whole. The teacher should also bear in mind that he is not only teaching a special skill, but that in the alchemy of growth what he teaches now will be transformed into some different quality in later years.

For instance, almost as soon as they come to school from the nursery class both girls and boys should learn to knit. This is a good training for the fingers in skilfulness, but it is far more than that. The rhythmical thinking with the fingers which knitting demands grows with the growing child, and when he grows up the man will think more cogently and more harmoniously because the child practised this skill just at the time when his first independent thinking was born.[1] Or, to take another example, the children will soon sew and embroider simple objects like bags, cushion-covers, cases for their flageolets, book-covers and so on. From the very first when they make their designs for decorating these objects they should understand that the design must always express the function. A book opens only at one side and has to be held one way up. A design for a book-cover should make this

[1] One of the most vigorous thinkers known to the author, who kindly read this book in MS., wrote that at the age of seven he had an illness which kept him in bed for a long time during which his constant occupation was knitting.

plain, so that anyone seeing a book lying on a table will instinctively take it up the right way. A bag opens only at the top. If it is made in a sequence of colours, the darker should be at the bottom, the lighter where it opens. Such things are not only important in themselves, they contain a seed for the future. How much of our architecture has either a design forced upon it irrespective of its use, or is purely functional and devoid of all artistic form. How few modern buildings have drawn a beauty of form out of the spiritual intention in their use. Great spiritual movements have always produced new and characteristic forms of architecture. Perhaps a new and living architecture is the surest sign that a new spiritual impulse is born.[2]

To return to the subject of needlework, when children are learning about foreign countries it is a fine thing for them to make and dress a number of dolls in national costume. When they are occupied with the study of animals, each child can make a stuffed animal—and it will be of great interest to see what animals different children choose. Such collections of dolls or animals may perhaps be given entire to the Nursery Class, or individually to younger children in the family. Children should be encouraged to *make* presents for birthdays and Christmas rather than buy them with their parents' money—a very easy operation.

After the twelfth year—keeping pace with the general curriculum—some fundamental technical skills should be learned. It is a good thing for both sexes to make an article of wearing apparel —perhaps shirts for the boys and blouses for the girls. It is especially good for the boys to discover how complicated the common shirt is. They will respect their shirts all the more when they have made one. Both boys and girls should learn darning and mending, and do some laundry and ironing. Even if they never have to exercise these arts in later life (though many of them will) it is good to understand the processes on which daily life depends. But even in the most practical matters the emphasis should be on the artistic. Childhood should recover the spirit of those great ages of handicraft when every object of common use flowered into some form of beauty.

It is not until this same twelfth year that children have sufficient

[2] The Goetheanum, built by Rudolf Steiner in Switzerland as the central School of Spiritual Science, is unique among modern buildings in being plastically conceived and executed.

control over their limbs and fingers to do serious work in woodwork or gardening. Naturally they will have played about with tools before and knocked together some simple practical objects. It is quite a different matter now that they begin to feel their bones and skeleton in the way already described. Then can now use a tool with some skill and accuracy. It need hardly be said that in a Waldorf School the first approach to serious woodwork is artistic rather than technical.

Most woodwork classes begin with such technical matters as the making of joints of all kinds, accurate measurement and designs prepared on paper. This is important in its own time and place, but an artistic approach sees rather the plastic possibilities of the material. If you make a box each side is conceived as flat, and only in fitting the parts together does the box enter three dimensions. But if you take a solid piece of wood and carve out of it, with chisel and rasp, a bowl or a boat or a door-handle or a candlestick, you are thinking and working in terms of three dimensions from the outset, and the experience both of the substance and of the form you create is quite different from the case of the box.

It is best for children to begin with the carving of some symmetrical form. A wooden spoon, a bowl, a scoop or a boat are all suitable objects, but a spoon is probably the easiest. Many a child will begin with the ambition to make a large stirring spoon, but by constant correction it will dwindle to a diminutive salt-spoon. For to make a symmetrical object is an exercise in thinking and judgment. To watch a child holding up his spoon or bowl and critically appraising it for symmetry is very much like hearing a judge weighing up both sides of a case. It is the dreamy children, whose thinking has not yet wakened, who find such an exercise in symmetry most difficult—and who therefore profit well by it.

After such exercises the children will pass on to the carving of free forms where balance rather than symmetry is required. When they do so, they should realise that the position as well as the use of an object should determine its form. A candlestick designed to stand on a mantelpiece has one relation to space: one intended for the centre of a table has another. The former should show by its form that it is designed to throw light in one direction only: the latter should be equally open to all directions. It is the same principle which we have seen guiding the design and colour in knitting and needlework.

Another healthy and artistic form of woodwork is the making of movable toys, especially if they are for younger brothers or sisters to play with. It is a way of introducing some imaginative charm into homes where often children get only ugliness or realism in their toys. Many of the toys will use the mechanical principles of wheel and lever about which the children are learning at this time. Perhaps a group of children can co-operate in making a rocking-boat or a play-house for a younger class. There should always be a balance between what is done individually and what is done in groups.

A systematic study of gardening can begin about the same time as woodwork, though here again the children will naturally have sown seeds and tended plants at home and school since they were quite little. But the sixth Grade should have, wherever possible, a garden of its own, in the working of which the children can learn the arts of growing both flowers and vegetables. If the school is in the country and possesses a farm there will be opportunities for farm-work as well, and especially for developing a true connection between farm and garden. The urban dweller is all too divorced from the soil, and it is a highly important thing to awaken in town children not only a love for but a practical knowledge of growing things. As a social task there are few better opportunities than gardening affords.

Many artistic activities, such as painting and modelling, which are separately pursued in other schools are integrated into the Main lesson in a Waldorf School and come within the sphere of the Grade Teacher. They are so essential a part of the imaginative approach to learning about the world that they could not and should not be divorced from the 'ordinary' lessons. When the children enter High School they will need specialist teachers for these subjects also. But the Grade Teacher prepares the way for the later art-work by fostering and educating the younger children's love of colour. The dominant impression of these children's paintings in a Waldorf School is clear and fluid colour. Form comes later, when it is born out of the interaction of the colours.

The musical education cannot be divorced in a Waldorf School from Eurhythmy, to which a special chapter is devoted. It is another of the elements which it is unlikely that the Grade Teacher will be able to supply. But he will fail in his duty to the children unless he is constantly aware of what they are doing in these other lessons, and is often present to observe their skill and their behaviour. Much can be learned by a teacher about his own children if he is able to watch them in other teachers' lessons. If problems of discipline arise with teachers who do not know the children so well, it must be the Grade Teacher's task to discover the cause and suggest the remedy. He is the natural Counsellor not only for the children but for their other teachers as well.

CHAPTER XV

Eurhythmy and Music

It may first of all be advisable to forestall confusion by stating that Eurhythmy—the art of movement initiated by Rudolf Steiner—is quite unconnected with the Eurhythmics of M. Jaques Dalcroze. The confusion of names is unfortunate and arose from the fact that the name Eurhythmics was not in force on the continent of Europe (though it was elsewhere) at the time when Steiner inaugurated and named Eurhythmy. Both these arts of movement (as their names imply) have an essential basis in rhythm: but beyond that their source of inspiration and their character are absolutely divergent.

If Steiner himself always laid the greatest stress on Eurhythmy in its three aspects—artistic, educational and curative—it was perhaps because it is the most immediate and practical expression of the contention central to his philosophy that man is the creation of spiritual powers and not essentially of physical forces. More than any other philosopher he has stressed and exemplified the Christian belief that the world is created by the divine *Logos,* called in the opening verse of St. John's Gospel 'the Word without which nothing was made which is made'. He therefore made a special study of the world of sound in the domains where it still possesses the last echo of its creative and formative power—the arts of music and of speech.

The first and most obvious distinction between Eurhythmy and other forms of movement is that it is expressive of speech as well as of music. For Steiner, language is not a conventional sound symbolism, as it is regarded by many modern anthropologists. The first words spoken by man were not modifications of primitive grunts. In his early dim picture-consciousness when man saw a tree or an animal or a flower the image awoke a corresponding movement within him. Sometimes the movement expressed itself in a gesture: but the human larynx is so formed that it enables man to make gestures in pure sound. It is such gestures of sound which are the foundations of language. There is a perfect picture of this birth of language in the Book of Genesis, where God is said to have brought all his creatures before Adam, 'and whatsoever Adam called every living creature, that was the name thereof'.

Our present languages are remote descendants of that innocent virginal speech. They have hardened into conventions and lost their plastic powers. It is remarkable that the more man develops a clever personal intelligence the less he is able to manipulate a mobile inflected language. The Eskimo, with his simple needs and primitive inventions, wields a far more complicated language with a much richer vocabulary than is spoken down the telephones of a modern office, or lives in the Babel of radio. Even the simpler distinctions of thought such as that between the indicative statement of fact (It *is* fine) and the problematical subjunctive (If it *be* fine) no longer find expression in the form of Western speech.

Nevertheless, rigid and conventional as our modern languages have become, the survival of poetry is alone ample evidence that they have not lost all their original creative force, nor have the ears of men grown entirely blunted to the significance of sound in creating and evoking meaning. In poetry meaning and sound are still in unity. It is commonly impossible to translate a poem from one language to another. When the sounds alter the meaning goes. The beauty of the variety of languages is that each language expresses an individual relationship not only to life in general but to everyday things. A tree is not the same to the French, the German and the English. The sounds of the names modify the experience.

It is on this *meaning of the sounds* that Eurhythmy is based. In speech every sound possesses a characteristic gesture which necessitates a particular movement of the larynx, and commonly goes no farther into the body. That it has a tendency to do so, however, is plain from the instinct—so strong among children and uninhibited peoples—to accompany speech with gesture. Eurhythmy is the conscious extension of this gesture in relation to pure sounds.

In the case of some sounds it is fairly easy to feel the immense difference of mood and picture which they evoke, and to let that mood or picture develop into movement. In the sound *O* we feel a containing force, something which holds, encloses and enfolds: the sound *Ah* on the other hand takes us out of ourselves into distant space—it is the sound with which we express wonder, as when we marvel at the beauty of the far-away stars. The movement in Eurhythmy for *O* is therefore the forming of a circle, generally with the entire arms and hands. The movement for *Ah* is to open the outstretched arms as though they would reach out to the far spaces in something of the mood which made an Indian astronomer once say to the amazement of a Western colleague: 'Sometimes I stretch out my hand and touch a star.'

The consonants affect us in a more external and pictorial manner—we see a rolling movement in the *rrr*, a darting in *fff*, a thrusting away in *ggg*, a conclusive gesture in *ttt*, and so on. We feel the inward quality of language in the vowels, while the consonants are more descriptive of outer things. This is why in all early scripts, where writing was still allied to the pictorial, the consonants only were written and the reader supplied the vowel sounds from his own intuition. The movements for the consonants in Eurhythmy are therefore more pictorial in character. In some cases they might almost be taken to imitate (as in mime) the thing to which a given word actually refers—for instance curved arms with finger-tips touching the head for the sound *T* in *tree*. In such a case, however, the resemblance is not due to external imitation, but to the fact that the same creative power of sound is still apparent in both the object and the word.

These are indications of the barest elements. It is a long discipline to live into the form and character of sound as Steiner did. But it will be seen what possibilities Eurhythmy possesses for awakening the will-element first in speech and then in thinking, and, on the other hand, for strengthening the consciousness of speech by bringing it into the sphere of bodily movement.

The sounds of music are no less creative and formative than the sounds of speech. If architecture has been called frozen music, the architecture of the human body may be called music become alive. Even the most rigid part of the body, the skeleton, is a symphony in harmony, number and proportion. The intervals of the simple scale produce as varied feelings as the pure sounds of speech. The second is like the first step into the world: we feel we cannot possibly stay at the point to which it brings us—it is bound to lead us elsewhere. Compare with its tentative mood the assertive quality of the fourth. No wonder Handel chose the fourth for the words, 'I know' in his setting of 'I know that my Redeemer liveth'. A modern composer (as an English musician once said) might easily choose the seventh for a setting of these words—and we would at once be quite certain that he was an agnostic and did *not* know! For of all intervals the seventh most creates the feeling of being scattered abroad. It is almost intolerable to hear a seventh constantly repeated or continuously sustained. The relief when its uncertainty is resolved by the assured octave is actually physical. We breathe again after feeling ourselves racked or torn asunder by invisible powers.

Nothing but the actual experience of learning and doing Eurhythmy can make real all that Steiner has revealed about music in the human body. The arm, for instance, is a visible expression of the intervals of the scale. Concentrate all your consciousness on the experience of the scale and allow it to bring your arms into motion. The interval of the second brings the first exploratory movement from the shoulder; it is felt in the upper arm. The third reaches the forearm with its far greater plastic possibilities given by the two bones—the radius and the ulna—which distinguish it so greatly from the upper arm. Here we may turn the arm more inwards—the experience of the minor interval—or outwards to the greater assurance of the major third. So we advance to the seventh which seems even to tear our finger-tips asunder: while the octave returns us to our base, not, however, with the initial potentiality which the tonic gave, but with the experience of the form of the whole arm. We discover that the scale is a venture into space and that, as in projective geometry, the farthest distance lies nearest to our home.

Even in the sphere of music, therefore, the basis of Eurhythmy is so different that its impact as an art cannot be compared with dancing or with mime. In the former, suitable movements accompany the rhythm of music, but they do not follow or express the form of the melody. In the latter, feelings and impulses evoked by the story are represented in gestures. Eurhythmy does neither of these things. It is more subtle than dance, more objective than mime, because it expresses in movement the actual cadence of a melody, the very sounds that make a poem. Like all true arts, it creates the laws by which it is bound.

We are here concerned with the educational value of Eurhythmy, however, and not immediately with its artistic purpose—though the two are not unrelated. It must be introduced to children by gradual stages. Young children should not be made too conscious in their movements. The precision of movement by which some dancing schools make little girls into accomplished ballerinas with all the tricks of the trade is to be heartily deplored. It has even been observed to produce a dullness of mind at a later age. In the Nursery Class and first Grades all movement is still by imitation, the children instinctively copying—some more and some less perfectly—the movements of the teacher. But already Eurhythmy can begin to play its part of handmaid to the other lessons. For the fairy-tales and fables which belong to this age can be brought into its life of movement. Was there not a fabulous fish and a tall tower by the sea in yesterday's fairy-tale? The Eurhythmy movement for the sound *ff* is the very image of the darting fish and that for *t* of the stern immobility of the tower. Did not a lion leap lightly over the fence in last week's fable? The gesture for the sound *l* will lead us to feel the movement as though we were the lion ourselves.

If we are going to perform a little story in this sort of eurhythmic acting, music must also come in. The children begin to feel the qualities of different rhythms—perhaps the light anapaest for the prince's horse galloping through the forest—the trochee for the princess lost at night in that same forest and thinking of the home she will never see again—the spondee for the ogre walking heavily home from his day's marauding. Picture, rhythm and feeling—when these are a unity and realised in movement, education has begun.

It is in the Eurhythmy lessons also that the foundations of geometry are laid. The children should walk and run—to music in varying rhythms—the forms of the square, pentagon, lemniscate, circle and so on. The figures then become something that they 'feel in their bones' and not merely carry in their heads. It is a social exercise too. If a number of children are walking the form of a pentagon—five perhaps for each side of the figure while another five follow the pentagram within the pentagon—every child must be in the right place at the right time, or confusion will result. There are certain Eurhythmy exercises accompanied by appropriate words such as 'We seek one another' which are specially designed to awaken a social sense through movement. No doubt the old formal dances—square dances, country dances, singing games and the like—instinctively performed something of the same function.

As the children grow older, more complicated movements to rhythm can be introduced. Perhaps they will mark the beat with their feet while they clap the rhythm with their hands—and then reverse the process. Or there will be rod exercises in which the exercise has its own rhythm and success depends on the exact timing of the movements, or your rod will clash with your neighbour's. These exercises are excellent for the control of the body, and for the development of concentration. It is instructive to see the gaucherie generally displayed by both child and adult beginners in such exercises—even if they are athletic and have a reputation for skill in games.

The characteristic stories and legends, on which the main lesson is essentially built, continue to provide admirable material for the Eurhythmy lessons, which in their turn enrich by movement the more intellectual content of the Main lesson. In the third Grade, when the children are studying the Old Testament stories, what could be more appropriate and wonderful than to take the opening chapter of Genesis and with great reverence portray in Eurhythmy movement all the marvellous creations of God: Light and Darkness, Sun, Moon and Stars, Waters above and Waters below, trees and herbs, great whales and winged fowl? Or to enact the part of Adam and give names to all the creatures that move on the earth?

The fourth class with its emphasis on the Norse Legends, and the fifth with the Greek Myths introduce the great difference in the basis of poetical rhythm between North and South. The alliterative metre of the North has a deep quality of will in it, and is an invigorating experience for the children as they emphasise in movement the repeated sounds, perhaps even of some original Anglo-Saxon. The hexameter, on the other hand, is the most harmonious, the most harmonising of all rhythms. In a sense its name 'six-metre' is misleading, for it has two silent feet as well as six spoken—the invariable break in the middle of the third foot, and the pause at the end of each line. Four beats with a silent breath on the last, and again four beats with a silent breath on the last—this is the hexameter rhythm. But it is also the rhythm which arises between the breathing and the heart—one breath to every four beats of the heart. If we picture the Greek bard holding the lyre against his heart, with the breath streaming from his lungs into the song, we can almost see the hexameter being created out of the central rhythm of human life.

It is therefore not only an educational but even a health-giving experience to bring the rhythm of the hexameter right into the movement of the limbs. Moreover, especially because the quantitative values of the hexameter—the contrast of long and short syllables, as opposed to the contrast of stressed and unstressed syllables on which English poetry is based—make it difficult to reproduce the true hexameter rhythm in English, nothing could be better than to take some of the actual lines of Homer. Their meaning can be explained in a general way, and, even if the children are not learning some of the elements of Greek, the interest they stimulate may awaken in some of them a desire to study the Greek language. You cannot be said to know ancient Greek without knowing the rhythm of the hexameter, and knowing a rhythm means a deeper experience than learning its laws in your head.

Many of the movements of Eurhythmy probably have the same kind of foundation as those of the Greek choral dance, examples of which remain on vases and in sculptures and bas-reliefs. Some of the Eurhythmy exercises, such as a beautiful form for the solemn Greek salutation *Evoe,* have, therefore, a special fitness in relation to the time when the children are studying Greek mythology and history.

The important changes in the twelfth year, the entry of the child's forces into the skeleton and the foreshadowing of the intellectual powers of puberty, are met and guided in the development of Eurhythmy. The child should now develop a greater control of his limbs: rod exercises, therefore, calling for a high accuracy of movement are introduced. On the other hand, his thinking power has made a leap forward: consequently the more intellectual element in speech—grammar—is stressed. Behind the abstract laws of grammar lies the reality of experience: we feel an active verb differently from a passive: the present tense differently from the future or past: indicative differently from subjunctive: an abstract noun differently from a concrete. Wherever there is a difference of feeling or experience, that difference creates in Eurhythmy a distinction in movement. To walk backwards requires much more conscious activity than to walk forwards: movement in a curve is not the same as in a straight line:

to go to the left is different from going to the right. Such distinctions of movement are used in Eurhythmy to mark the fundamental forms of speech. For children who find grammar difficult, movement is often the awakener of the understanding: for those who find it easy, movement gives it a new reality: for all it is a wholesome experience and gives meaning to the statement of the great medieval grammarian, John of Salisbury, that without grammar a man cannot be truly healthy.

At this age, when the children begin to take possession of the entire body even as far as the skeleton, musical Eurhythmy, like a modern Amphion, should be called on to assist in the building. For the completion of the body means that a new microcosm is created, reflecting the powers of the twelve zodiacal signs, and the forces of the seven planets. In music this is the experience of the whole scale, which—not without reason—possesses its seven fundamental tones and the five accidentals, which make twelve notes in all. In Eurhythmy therefore it is now the whole scale which is brought into play: the children should begin to perform simple pieces of music using the movements for all the intervals. It is excellent if in this Grade—and indeed in all Grades—some of the children play on flute, violin and cello while the rest perform the Eurhythmy.

All these exercises are continued in the seventh and eighth Classes. Contrasting moods are now especially emphasised. Ballads provide excellent material with their quick dramatic movement, their humour and their tragedy. They also contain much of the feeling of wish, wonder and surprise to which the children's attention is drawn in the grammar lessons of the seventh Class.[1]

The impact of Eurhythmy will be all the greater if there is the closest possible co-operation between the Class teacher and the Eurhythmy teacher. The former will learn much about his children if he goes regularly into the Eurhythmy lessons and observes how they move. Special exercises can be devised to meet some new problem or mood in the class, the choice of suitable poems and music can be made together, a child with some individual difficulty can be given a particular part in a ballad or an exercise. When the Eurhythmy teacher is as much interested in what the children are learning in their main lessons, as the Class

[1] See p. 134.

teacher in what they are doing in movement, the children thrive in a harmony of mind and will.

In the High School age the boys will at first prefer exercises which require skill and dexterity: the girls will be far more ready to express their feelings in movement. There is therefore the need for greater differentiation. But Eurhythmy is still the handmaid of the main lessons. In the ninth and tenth Classes, for instance, it reflects and reinforces much of the literature lessons. Movements for different rhythms and stanza forms can be worked out. The character and mood of a poem may be expressed—thoughtful, emotional, inspiriting, didactic, elegiac or what you will. Some poetry is more Apolline, some more Dionysian. In fact all that the children learn in the tenth Grade about the art of poetry can be prepared, illustrated and confirmed in Eurhythmy.

In music the advance is made from melody to harmony. Different chords—so different in their effect—call for different movements. The children should now experience the harmonic structure of a piece of music, as well as the melody. When the eleventh Grade brings a special study of the history of music, harmony has an important place. A composer is known in his characteristic harmonies. In all this Eurhythmy confirms the impress of the special work of the year.

In the last two Grades some really artistic work can be done, in which much will depend on the children, the teacher and the school. It is a specially happy thing if Eurhythmy can be used in a social way, perhaps in a play when there are nature-spirits, as in Milton's *Comus*, or *A Midsummer-Night's Dream*; or for the chorus of a Greek play; or for the celebration of a seasonal Festival.

Of all elements in modern life it is the rhythmical side which is most deficient—a deficiency only too apparent in the arts today. The whole of a Waldorf education is based on rhythm, and may therefore be called curative for an age. But in this rhythmical education there is no doubt where the centre lies. It is in Eurhythmy.

* * *

Singing lessons are happily a major feature in all good schools today and choirs and orchestras reach astonishing standards. A

Waldorf School should certainly not lag behind in these activities—indeed the first school in Stuttgart was a pioneer in several practices which have since become common—but it is in Eurhythmy that it makes its most novel contribution to musical education. The ideal for music in general would be that all children should both play an instrument and be able to read a part in round or madrigal, as our Elizabethan ancestors are credibly allowed to have done.

In the first classes the songs cannot be too simple or too tuneful. Minor tunes, with their greater inwardness, need not be introduced till the fourth Grade, but by the third the children should be writing airs in the scale of C major. In every singing lesson there should also be some listening to music; and, as every child from the first Grade onwards plays a flageolet, it will soon be possible to have voices accompanied by wind, in unison at first and then in canon or in parts.

The playing of flageolets gives a good indication of a child's musical ability, and will be helpful in deciding on an orchestral instrument. For, unless a child shows outstanding ability for the piano, he will ultimately benefit far more by learning an orchestral instrument through all the opportunities it gives for making music with others. It will be especially useful to take the child's temperament into account in selecting an instrument.[2] Many children lose heart and detest the necessary practice because the instrument chosen is not suitable to them.

If the study of different instruments begins with the third or fourth Grade, the eighth should see the development of a small orchestra to accompany the singing in several parts which will also have been achieved by this time. The main School Orchestra and Choir will be invaluable for all festival occasions. But they are inevitably always losing their leading members and require a constant influx of new recruits. The Junior or Class orchestra and choir is therefore not only valuable in itself but as a training-ground for the future. To keep a school orchestra constantly in balanced strength requires much foresight.

In the High School the curriculum includes a special period of lessons on the development and appreciation of music. Naturally, however, the children will already be familiar with many composers and have had many opportunities of hearing music and

[2] See the chapter on The Temperaments.

about music before this time. For in this age, when every home resounds with radio, it is imperative to give children frequent opportunities of hearing the living sound of real instruments. The custom of explaining pieces just before performance—as though children would not otherwise be interested—should be avoided. In the right place and time they can learn about the form of a piece of music, the themes and their development, the use of the different instruments and so on. But all this can easily cast an intellectual veil over the true experience of the music. Dissection and analysis should be forgotten in the pure enjoyment of a work of art. Children can be prepared the week before to understand what they are going to hear. But at the actual concert the music should speak for itself—and speak to the heart more than to the head.

When all is said and done, however, the musical life of a school may turn out to be nothing more than a valuable side-line or relaxation, not related to the main work and teaching. A Waldorf School believes that education in music is chiefly valuable when it forms part of a musical education. In a modern form and spirit it echoes Plato's words in the *Republic*: 'We attach supreme importance to musical education, because rhythm and harmony sink most deeply into the recesses of the soul and take most powerful hold of it, bringing gracefulness in their train and making a man graceful if he be rightly nurtured, but if not the reverse.' The gracefulness to which Plato refers is not only aesthetic: it is the ground of reason and morality. It seeks for harmony in nature, and harmony in the soul. It is to this search that a Waldorf education is dedicated; it may therefore truly be called a musical education.

CHAPTER XVI

The Temperaments

It was Steiner's habit to graft the results of his spiritual researches on to whatever worthy stock he found in earlier forms of knowledge. In the process he developed and altered no doubt, but he brought over some of the riches of past ages into the forms of modern perception, and he entirely avoided the arrogance which implies, even if it does not actually claim, that knowledge began with the birth of modern Natural Science and Psychology. His terminology alone is proof of his connection with the past. He talked about the Soul, when only the Psyche was allowed to exist: and when at one time life brought him into contact with the Anglo-Indian theosophists, he adapted many terms of ancient Hindu wisdom to his own use.

It is natural therefore that, when he dealt with those human types which lie between the individual and man in general, he linked what he had to say to the traditional Greek and medieval classification of the Temperaments.

This classification is generally regarded by modern psychologists as naïve, and they have supplanted it with many acute divisions. The fact is, it is possible to divide men into almost any number of psychological types. But they lose their practical use through their very subtlety and variety. The Temperaments are concerned with broader-bottomed distinctions.

The psychological type is generally based on the faculty which the individual uses in his mental and emotional response to the world. Thus Jung posits four such types who express themselves characteristically through thinking or feeling or sensation or intuition. But penetrating each of these types he recognises the overriding distinction of the extrovert and the introvert. For you may direct any of these faculties equally to the outside world or to the inner life of your mind. In this division according to 'manner of use' Jung comes closest to the kind of fundamental distinction that Steiner sought for in the Temperaments, a distinction which penetrates to the depth of the human being. George Meredith once maintained that nothing is true unless you can write a poem about it. He meant that nothing is true unless it is rooted in those depths of Nature and Human Nature from which poetry springs. It is hard to imagine a poem about an extrovert sensation type. But it is not hard to imagine one about the temperaments. John Milton wrote two such poems, on how the sanguine man and the melancholic man would wish to spend their day. They are called *L'Allegro* and *Il Penseroso,* and it is difficult to imagine purer examples of poetry.

The Temperaments have always been held to have a very definite physiological basis. The fact that a temperament was called a 'humour' takes us immediately into the heart of Greek and medieval medicine which was so much concerned with the fluid processes in the body. The very names of the temperaments were taken from the fluid—blood, phlegm or bile—which was at once their physical expression and their cause. There was no distinction then between physiology and psychology.

Steiner did not follow medieval physiology or psychology in its detail. On the contrary he always maintained that the relation between soul and body has altered during the centuries. But he was thoroughly in agreement with the conception of the physical basis of temperament as an example of the intimate reciprocity between body and soul.

The temperament then is more than a matter of the psyche, it penetrates into the physical constitution as well. It is to be recognised in build and gait and complexion: it affects health and disease: it distinguishes whole peoples as well as individuals: it marks different ages of life.

To explore the ultimate basis of temperament in full is beyond the scope of a book on education, but it is important to touch on it sufficiently to indicate why there are four and not three or seven temperaments. It will at the same time help to show why Steiner attached so much importance to them. For the temperament is the mediator between what is individual in man and what is generic. In Steiner's view it is the latter only which properly lies in the domain of inheritance. From our parents we obtain the characteristics of humanity as exemplified in a particular stock or family—though it has been pointed out that family likeness especially may often be the consequence of imitation. But into this domain of heredity there enters the individual spirit which existed before birth and will survive death. The temperament is concerned with the particular mode of adjustment made between the hereditary and individual principles. Why then is it fourfold? The answer can only be given by making explicit the fourfold nature of the human being which has been implicit throughout this book.

From our parents we inherit not only our physical body, which taken alone would be no more than the mineral element in us, but also the forces of life which penetrate it, and without which it would disintegrate as the corpse disintegrates after death. We receive therefore a double inheritance from our parents, a purely physical body and what—for want of a better term—we can call a life-body. It is notable that in the former the father, in the latter the mother, generally plays the greater part, which is the reason why a child can perform the astonishing feat of resembling both his parents, however different the two may be.

From the side of Individuality also we must recognise two principles as uniting with the parent-created embryo which is at first only physical and life-body. We have already distinguished the spheres of consciousness and self-consciousness, which mark the absolute division between man and animal, and we have called them the 'consciousness-body' and the 'ego'. The latter could not exist without the former, but the former though individualised (as in the case of the animal) through entering a particular body, is not yet individual. Neither are necessary to the life processes of an organism—indeed the less they are present the greater are the powers of recuperation and survival, as in the lower forms of animal life. During sleep they leave the organism, which repairs its wastage all the better for their absence. But in man's waking life the consciousness-body and the ego have to integrate themselves into the physical and life-bodies which are the generic gift of heredity. In life there is never an absolute balance and it will practically always prove the case that one or other of these principles or 'bodies' will predominate over the others. It is this predominance which determines the temperament, and it follows from the fact that there are four 'principles' that there are also four temperaments.[1]

[1] This is the simplest account of the basis of the temperaments, and the one which Rudolf Steiner generally gave. He emphasised, however, that in children the nature and the interrelation of the principles is somewhat different. The characteristics of the temperaments, however, are the same.

To express it very briefly, if the inmost centre of a man's being, his ego, overrides the other principles, he will be choleric, with great energy and great tenacity. If the 'consciousness body' prevails over the others and escapes from the strong control of the ego, there will be a constant awareness of changing sense-impression or of the undirected flow of ideas. Such a man will have much interest in many things, but it will be shallow and fickle. He will be sanguine. If the life processes are all-important, producing the comfortable complacency, which rightly follows a good dinner, as the characteristic mood of man's life, he will not take a vivid or abiding interest in anything in the world around him except what conduces to his own well-being. He will be phlegmatic. If the physical body outweighs everything else, so that the ego is doomed to be perpetually overcoming, or failing to overcome, a certain weight and resistance in reaching the outside world, and is therefore driven back upon itself, the melancholic temperament will result.

Every temperament has some special virtues, but if any one temperament gains too violent a hold on the personality, a dangerous lack of balance may result. All the temperaments have both their lesser dangers and their greater. The choleric child may suffer from nothing worse than the fits of anger and passion to which so many children are subject: but these fits may degenerate into an actual mania. The changeableness of the sanguine may slide over into lunacy. The lack of interest which the phlegmatic shows can become a state of vacant idiocy. The melancholic's moods of depression may produce delusions such as persecution manias. Our asylums are filled with people whose temperament has grown too strong for them.

Anyone who has been in a company where drunkenness is prevalent will have noticed how markedly the temperament appears when a man is drunk. One man will get fighting drunk: another will be sentimental and maudlin: a third will become hilarious: a fourth vacant and sodden. It was an old tradition in army circles that you do not know a man until you have known him drunk—and to the extent that drunkenness reveals the temperament the tradition has some truth in it.

When we consider the number of people today who spend some part of their lives in a mental home, many of them as a result of the degeneration of temperament, we can see how important it is to treat the temperament in childhood in such a way that the adult is able to be its master and not its slave. There is only one way to do this. A child with a marked temperament must be allowed to give full reign to it and play it out. It is useless to try to force him to be the opposite of what he is. He will only fall deeper in the mire.

If we make an ideal description of each temperament it must not be imagined that many children will be found to conform to all or even many of its characteristics. For most children, like most adults, have a mixed temperament. A sanguine child will often have many phlegmatic traits. The melancholic equally frequently has a fund of hidden choler. It is even possible to be markedly of one temperament in one domain of life and of another in another. Generally, however, the temperament colours the whole man and nearly always the whole child. It is something of an art to recognise a temperament, akin to the perception by which a connoisseur recognises the author of a painting or of a piece of music. But one has to begin with the broader contrasts.

Imagine a child, then, sturdily, even stockily built, who walks as though he wanted to drive his heels into the ground at every step. His head is set well down on his shoulders, his eyes are dark and burning—perhaps jet-black—and his hands reflect his general build, a stout fist and strong fingers which hold a tool firmly and capably. He is deeply interested in the world, especially in what men do in it, and when he takes up a task he sees it through to the end. He wants to be a leader in everything and other children recognise his supremacy and gladly follow him. 'Let me play the lion too,' is his cry. For he is choleric, like Bottom the Weaver, and pushes himself forward on every occasion. Tom Sawyer is an admirable picture of a healthy choleric boy.

He is a great asset to the class which like all mankind needs leaders, and his tenacity helps to carry it along and keep it interested. But his abounding energy must be given scope and direction. In a play he must have a very active and magnificent part, and in general he should be given difficult work and left to cope with the difficulties himself. Perhaps the teacher will have to find him some regular heavy task—and this is not easy in a modern school where there is no wood to chop, no coals to cart and no heavy polisher for the floors. If you need to quieten him, describe a scene of even greater violence and excitement and heroism than he can himself imagine and let him see—in a story—that you can get immensely and violently angry. If he is inclined to be cock-a-hoop, let him perform some task in front of the class—and then praise the other children for taking so much interest. Do not seat him next to a melancholic child, who will only annoy him and whom he will frighten out of his wits. Put him next to another choleric, and then if he punches he will get punched in turn. Above all you must endeavour to capture his admiration and loyalty, and this you will do best if you can show him that you are a person of skill and capacity. For the choleric longs to achieve things himself, and will immediately respect achievement in others.

Picture another child, more slightly built, with finer bones and a springing almost dance-like walk. His neck is rather long, his eyes are blue and he often has a mop of curly hair. When he is working he will turn round at the smallest noise. His cupboard at home is full of things he has begun and never finished. His interest is easily caught and he is as eager to answer a question as the choleric, waving his arm in the air to catch the teacher's attention, as though it were a windmill. But he may even have forgotten the question and the answer before it is his turn to speak, and he will certainly not remember them the next day. For his mind is the soil without depth of earth on which the sower's seed grows quickly but withers as fast. He is the sanguine child, and he is the most typical of all children. For every age of life has its temperament, and childhood has an overriding sanguine temperament which generally prevents the other temperaments from coming to the same intense expression as with the adult.

From the sanguine children the teacher can learn much about childhood. He will discover from them the imperative need of holding the children's attention by liveliness and variety. They will teach him never to stick rigidly to a prepared lesson, but to give free play to the changing genius of the hour, pursuing the absorbing topic which has unexpectedly arisen, and yet at the end returning to his muttons. He will learn to forgive them when they desert the promised task, or burst into laughter at some trivial incident when he had hoped to produce a mood of solemnity. More than the other children they will show him how ridiculous he is. When he wants quick interest, or the escape of laughter, or a change of mood, he can turn to his most sanguine children and they will lead the class.

It is good to give the sanguine children a great variety of tasks, and change them, perhaps faster even than they want—provided the tasks are not too serious. But it will nearly always be possible to find that a sanguine child has one interest in which he is not sanguine but shows much tenacity. This interest should be encouraged by every possible means. For just because it is the temperament of childhood, the sanguine possesses the greatest danger for children, especially in an age which has invented every form of distraction alike for child and adult. It is the one temperament which should be countered by directly encouraging its opposite as well as by giving it a free rein. Sanguine children have also one other important characteristic. Because they are children *par excellence* they need to attach themselves in love to some adult, who is the anchor and compass of their mobile world. They will then perform tasks through love for their teacher and their desire to win his approval which their temperament would otherwise preclude. The Grade Teacher especially should find ways of fostering the love of sanguine children, just as he should impress the cholerics with his ability.

Let us pass to another type of child. Imagine a girl, slender and graceful, with brown eyes, or perhaps grey like Pallas Athene's, smooth hair and long fingers. She walks rhythmically and rather deliberately and all her movements are controlled. She enjoys her own company more than most children, and her possessions are generally tidy and in good order. In class she often seems to go into a 'brown study' and you would say she is not listening. But next day she will ask you an interesting question about what you said, which shows that you had more of her attention than you thought. She is the melancholic child, and like the melancholy Jacques in *As You Like It*, when the conversation has long moved on she will still be 'harping on the seventh cause'.

She is generally the delight of teachers. For she is receptive, reflects on what she learns, has original ideas and asks intelligent questions. But she is shy of speaking and must be encouraged before she will tell her thoughts. Whatever she does she does carefully. When the class is painting, she will still be working at one corner when the sanguine children have tossed off two or three negligent masterpieces. Her favourite colour is blue or mauve and she shrinks from the startling reds in which the cholerics rejoice. When the teacher wants an example of thoughtful work, or wishes to recall some lesson long past or to evoke a mood of sympathy and compassion, he can turn to his melancholics.

The melancholic sounds the ideal child, and indeed adults generally prefer him (for of course he may be a boy) because he occupies himself and gives little trouble. But he can be difficult to handle. He can easily become very sorry for himself because of some imagined injustice, or simply because life is too much for him, and he may well be selfish and unsocial. He shrinks from any sudden proposal, and will refuse to go to the party he inwardly longs to attend. He must be prepared for a social even some days ahead. Tell him that in six days' time there will be that wonderful party and he will just be setting off to enjoy himself. Remind him which of his friends will be there and what he will especially like. Repeat the process every day, and there is good hope that he will go quite cheerfully when the time comes. And how he will delight to tell you all about it afterwards! When he is sorry for himself, as he often is, it is fatal to go up to him with cheery words of encouragement. Tell him stories, suitable to his age, of the troubles and trials of other people, and in sympathy with theirs he will forget his own. In a tactful way the teacher should let him know that he too has had his disappointments and difficulties, and has struggled to overcome them. Thus he will win his sympathy, and with it his respect and confidence.

Lastly, we must picture that rather rare child—the phlegmatic. He is fat and dumpy, with a round and rather expressionless face, and he has 'no speculation in his eye'. He is quite content to be left alone, and will even go on sitting in his seat when the whole class has gone out to recess or to another lesson, because 'nobody told me to go'. He seems to take very little interest in any of his lessons and very rarely contributes. He is fond of his food, likes to eat candy and sleeps heavily. The Fat Boy in *The Pickwick Papers* ('Drat that boy, he's asleep again') is a good example of the phlegmatic. To some extent he is asleep even when he is awake and you have to rattle on his desk when you want his special attention for something. You can stir him into activity by outdoing him at his own game. Tell him a story very slowly, with long pauses between each word, and in as monotonous a voice as you can assume. After a time he will show signs of discomfort, and start fidgeting in his chair (an unusual sign of activity); if you then break off and ask him a question he will answer quite vigorously. It is no small thing to extract even this amount of energy from him.

But there is one point where his energy can be aroused. He likes to watch what the other children are doing. This is a great virtue and should be encouraged in every possible way. Do not ask him to repeat something from yesterday's lesson, as you would ask a melancholic, but get him to tell you what Dick painted or Jane modelled or Ruth acted or Harry showed to the class. For he really cares for the other children, and through this can be stimulated to a fine unselfishness, and to activity as well. If another child hurts himself it is the phlegmatic child who will tend him and lead him away to be dressed and bandaged. For there is much of the brooding motherly quality in this temperament. A phlegmatic girl especially can become a little mother to the whole class. Perhaps in the end the phlegmatic can become the greatest of temperaments, because by sympathy and attention it can imbibe the virtues of them all. But, of course, by then it has ceased to be phlegmatic!

It has been mentioned that it is a good practice to seat a choleric child next to another of his own kind. The same is true of all the temperaments. A phlegmatic will be bored by his phlegmatic neighbour and stimulated to some activity, just as a choleric will encounter opposition and become somewhat subdued. If all the children of like temperament are seated together, the class will resemble an orchestra, with compact groups of strings, woodwinds, brass and percussion. And it is as an orchestra that a teacher should think of his class, commanding and enjoying to the full the virtues and tones of all his human instruments.

A knowledge of the temperaments is a great help in preparing a subject to present to the children. For there will always be some aspect which will appeal more to one temperament than to the other, so that diversity of a healthy kind can be brought into the lesson. In mathematics, for instance, the sanguine children will glory in big numbers and delight in those sums where the amounts grow larger by leaps and bounds, as in the story of the man who paid the blacksmith five cents for the first nail in his horse's shoes, ten for the second, twenty for the third and so on —and there were forty-eight nails altogether. The melancholics will prefer it when amounts get steadily smaller and smaller, as when a gang of men are planting out young trees and every day there are nine less rows to plant. The choleric can be asked to work out how much work each labourer will have to do if there are thirty thousand trees to plant in twelve days and there are eight men. In any subject dealing with human affairs it will generally be evident what aspect of it will appeal to each temperament. If you are taking the story of Columbus, who will be most interested in the difficulties he had to overcome and his immense tenacity of purpose? Who will feel most for the tragic end of his story, both for himself and for the peoples he discovered? Who will like to picture island after island with the inhabitants bringing their gifts to the white men in their floating houses? And who will like to think of the homes of the islanders, what they ate and how they cooked it? Or again, from what different points of view you can approach the tremendous story of the French Revolution: the miseries of the down-trodden peasants: the succession of vivid scenes from the march of the women on Versailles to the whiff of grapeshot: the republican ideals which link Valley Forge to Varennes: the tremendous career of Napoleon.

But it is not in history alone that distinctions can be made according to the temperaments. In the first grammar lessons it is the choleric children who will be most attracted to the verbs and love to come out and act them: the melancholics will appreciate the fine distinctions of quality which are expressed by the adjectives: the sanguine children will be interested in the nouns as representing the variety of objects which can be found in some particular place, a wood or a stream or the seashore. For children the world is still so much a picture of man that many other subjects also can be treated in accordance with temperament. Different animals, different plants and trees, even different parts of plants—root, leaf, flower and fruit—will interest different kinds of children.

It will be specially valuable to consider the temperament in giving children individual work to do, both at home and at school. Children are not always wise enough to know what they will in fact find the most interesting pursuit. Their judgment is too much based on imitation and other irrelevant factors to be reliable. To suggest to a child his reading, his hobby, his musical instrument according to his temperament is often to make the difference between boredom and enthusiasm. It is a difference well worth the making.

After the uniformity of teaching common in the schools of the nineteenth century, the twentieth has seen a strong swing to individual instruction in small classes and study rooms. It is highly doubtful, however, whether this century has produced as many outstanding individual characters as the last. The fact is that too much individual instruction can easily press too hard on the child who becomes set when he should still be plastic, and self-reliant before he has developed a self to rely on. A child needs a certain freedom to assimilate what he can when he can, and he does not always want counsellors inspecting him to see if he is sufficiently challenged or if he ought to repeat this or that subject. That is why a Waldorf School is content to have much larger classes than in other modern forms of education. But through the temperaments it brings variety into the class without disintegrating it into units. A knowledge of the temperaments is an immense educational asset to the teacher as well as of the highest benefit to the child.

For if a child can overcome his temperament by working it off in childhood there are hopes that he will be able to achieve the ideal of commanding at will the virtues of all the temperaments. There are occasions in life—cocktail parties and the like—when a man can properly put on a sanguine temperament. If he has to drive through a congested city, he will do well to practise the patience of the phlegmatic. When some ideal has to be fought for, he should take the untiring sword of the choleric. For his inner life of philosophy or religion he needs the meditative depth of the melancholic.

In the wisdom of the older world the temperaments were always associated with the four elements, earth, water, air and fire, which is only another way of speaking of the four bodies or principles whose intermixture we have seen as the cause of temperament. The harmonious mixture of the elements therefore made the ideal man. It is as such that Mark Antony describes Brutus, 'the noblest Roman of them all', at the end of Shakespeare's *Julius Caesar*. For of Brutus he says that the elements were:

> So mixed in him that Nature might stand up
> And say to all the world, 'This was a man.'

CHAPTER XVII

Adolescence

PUBERTY divides childhood from adolescence as effectively as the Alps separate the sunny slopes and plains of Italy from the harsher climate of the North. It is so obvious a barrier that little need be said of its chief external characteristics. Even in the realm of physiology, however, it is Steiner's view that it is not alone or essentially in the development of the sexual organs that the most important physical changes of this time are to be sought. The formative processes which were so active in the head in the early years of life have now reached the limbs. Legs and arms of boys grow out of sleeves and trousers and become for a time unmanageable. Both sexes frequently outgrow their strength. At the same time the forces of awareness and 'awakeness', which animated the young child so vividly in his limbs, have worked up to the head and the first independent intellectual and critical thinking begins.

It is an age at which a teacher should watch his children narrowly for signs of over-strain or exhaustion. It is easier at this age, perhaps, than any other to develop the critical faculty prematurely with much ultimate detriment both to the child's health and to his mind. An even greater liveliness of teaching, a richer imagination, a warmer enthusiasm is needed now than formerly. The more the children's attention can be directed from themselves to the world, the more harmoniously will they pass through this often difficult phase of development.

Seen from another point of view, puberty is the climax of the process of incarnation—that is, the climax of childhood. The child achieves the last physical accomplishment, the ability to produce his kind. In nothing is man more different from the animal than in the results of puberty—in the animal, maturity and absorption into his species: in man the beginning of new mental powers and the appearance of unsuspected traits of individuality. But, physically speaking, the child stands on the earth at puberty, a mature member of the human race.

It is perhaps the least attractive period of childhood. The child has lost the innocent wayward fantasy of his earlier years and has not achieved the idealism of youth. The principal Art Inspector of the British Ministry of Education once told the teachers of a Rudolf Steiner School that there is no art at this age. Even if it requires qualification, this is a significant statement. For art is the perception of the qualitative as opposed to the utilitarian. Vast numbers of men and women in our modern civilisation never recover this art, which they lost with puberty. It is remarkable that the word 'proletarian'[1] was originally applied to the class who could reproduce their kind, and do practical work, but had no other value for society. Its members never advanced beyond the utilitarian stage of puberty.

Unfortunately in our modern technical schools adolescent education continues to derive from the same utilitarian outlook. Even if it is technically educated, the bulk of our population remains a proletariat.

All this has been alluded to in former chapters. It is now time to take up the theme again in greater detail and from fresh considerations.

Compared with the change of teeth, which marks the beginning of the middle period of childhood, the change of puberty, which ends it, is a far more complicated process. The pictorial thinking which is born with the change of teeth appears simple and objective when contrasted with all those realisations and self-realisations which arise when the whole inner world of thought awakens to enchant and trouble the astonished adolescent. Further, the change of teeth shows the same characteristics in boys and girls: the effects of puberty are different in the two sexes both in time and character. Indeed it is impossible to understand puberty without investigating some of the fundamental differences between man and woman.

Those psychologists are undoubtedly right who find much difference between the sexes in children even at a very early age. Little girls have commonly a feeling for clothes entirely absent in the boy, while the boy's early interest in the mechanical is seldom shared by the girl.[2] The mistake, however, is to connect,

[1] From Latin *proles*, meaning *offspring*.

[2] A small girl of four, expecting the arrival of a boy cousin, once asked the author in her cot at night: 'What shall I put on tomorrow for Philip to see me in?'—a kind of question which would hardly occur to the male mind before the adolescent age of 'dating'.

equate or confuse such differences with the erotic experience of sex. There is an overriding distinction between man and woman of which the modern *eros* forms no essential part. It is a distinction which no science of man can understand unless it can re-establish the old religious tradition of the Fall of Man.

The consequences of the Fall and its reflection in the lives of children have already been discussed in their relation to the development of consciousness and self-consciousness. Through the Fall man received knowledge of the world and of himself before he was responsible or moral enough to support it—a state of affairs never more apparent than at the present day. But it is through incarnation that man develops from consciousness to self-consciousness in his life on earth. In the case of individuals it is easy to observe that one person is more deeply incarnated, more 'on the earth'—to use a common phrase—than another. In a more subtle, but not less intelligible manner, the male sex as a whole is more deeply impressed and incarnated in the physical body than the female. Puberty, therefore, is a slower because a deeper process with the boy than with the girl.

Many of the more common differences between men and women are explicable in these terms. It is generally true, for instance, that men, being more deeply incarnated, find it harder than women to interest themselves in spiritual matters or in religion; while women, being less incarnated, are not so fitted by nature to such severely practical pursuits as engineering or industrial chemistry. There is, however, more to be observed at puberty than merely the depth of incarnation.

Up to adolescence the thought life of children has been naturally objective, it has been *given to them* in the same way as their vitality, their likings and dislikings, their impulses to do this or that. After puberty—and this is the all-important distinction—they begin to find the source of their thoughts in their own inner life. The stage of the individual child at this time may be compared to the change in social history from a traditional patriarchal monarchy to a city-state making its first blundering endeavours to formulate its own laws. It is a tremendous moment when a child first realises that he has an inner world of thought, feeling and sensation which is his own peculiar treasure, for which he is alone responsible, and to which no one else on earth can say *Open Sesame.*

It is just because she does not advance so deeply into physical incarnation that this new subjective world is more accessible to the girl than to the boy. She is more at home in it, she expresses herself more readily in the forms with which it provides her. She reveals her new inner life more naturally and gracefully, both in her general behaviour and in the avowal of her ideals. The boy, on the other hand, is driven into deeper connection with the outer physical world and finds it harder to come to terms with his own inner life. His physical gaucherie finds its counterpart in his apparently philistine mentality. He instinctively conceals what the girl instinctively reveals.

The two states have naturally their appropriate degradations. The inwardness of the girls may easily degenerate into the horrors of backbiting and spitefulness; the externalism of the boys into the frightfulness of bullying and organised cruelty. Not least among the advantages of co-education is that, rightly directed, it can help to correct the one tendency by the other. The girls feel the contempt of the boys for their cattishness, the boys feel the horror of the girls at their loutishness. To enjoy the good opinion of the other (which they both secretly covet) each party somewhat amends its ways.

In this distinction at puberty we are witnessing the genesis of that fruitful difference between men and women on which much might be built for the betterment of social life if it were properly understood, whereas the failure to understand it is often the cause of much unhappiness. The man's gift is to understand the objective by the process of logic; the woman's to apprehend the subjective by the process of intuition. A man listens to what someone says and is interested in the precise meaning of his words: a woman is more concerned with why the man says it and what he really means.

She feels more the social and psychological implications of what is said, while the man limits himself to the content. She listens to the spirit, he to the letter. The logical man stands helpless and indignant before the woman's assertion: 'You ought to have known what I really meant.' The intuitive woman is baffled and exasperated by the crude literalness of the man.

Both faculties are valuable and should be used in social life. One example may be given from Steiner's works on social questions. The man is essentially gifted for inventions—there are very few women inventors, though women have probably the greater genius in 'making do'. But when an invention has been made, there is the no less important question of how it shall be established in life, a matter which in the past has been notoriously left to chance. It requires a different genius from that of the inventor to foresee the social implications of the invention, and to prevent, or at least minimise, the distress and chaos which its intrusion into the established order of things may cause. It is in foresight of this kind that the woman's natural genius might well outclass the man's.

We must return, however, to the adolescent. It is important to realise that both boys and girls are often desperately shy of their new inward life, and endeavour to hide their shyness in different and characteristic fashion. When a girl is volubly indignant against the injustices with which she or her friends have been treated, the wise teacher will realise that the explosion is partly to distract her own attention from some sense of weakness or failure which is haunting her conscience. When a boy appears to find his only pleasure in playing the fool, he may perhaps be writing poetry about which he speaks to no one. The teacher's cue is to let both see that he does not take their attitude too seriously—and, without moralising, to present them with ideas for life. It is excellent to discuss with them quite practically the career they have in mind and to point out the opportunities it may give for something more than making a living. If some outstanding personality is described it will be a fruitful policy to discuss his character with the boys, and with the girls to emphasise his work and deeds. It will help to balance the one-sided tendencies of the two. For though it is generally the right and sensible thing to work with the natural tendencies of childhood and not against them, it should never be forgotten that the ultimate aim is the balanced life and not the one-sided: it is always good to prepare the ground for the opposite crop which will only mature later. Broadly speaking, girls in adolescence are more open to the appeal of the beautiful. 'Beauty is truth, truth beauty' has a deep significance for them. For boys, the need is practical heroism—even the heroism that brings alert senses and strong muscles. '*Laborare est orare*' in its obvious sense represents their best philosophy. Perhaps they will discover later that prayer is only prayer when it has the strenuousness of work, and work is only work when it has the earnestness of prayer.

It would be a happy thing if the general change and development at puberty could be found of such interest and importance that what is commonly called the sex question could be forgotten. But the question has become of such immense importance in certain schools of thought that some reference to it must be made. An indication has already been given of the broad physiological field of which a knowledge of conception and birth forms a natural part.[3] Most modern children are aware of the nature of birth, if not of conception, before the twelfth year. The special opportunity of the school—in this as in much else—is to give the right setting and tone to the knowledge the children may have acquired. The danger in modern frankness over questions of birth and sex is that with the information the children insensibly imbibe materialism. The child asks: 'Where did I come from?' The parent answers: 'Out of your mother's body', and never realises that he has equated 'body' and 'I'—an equation which the Buddha, Socrates, Boëthius, Aquinas (and a good many other wise men) were at some pains to deny. To those who believe in the incarnation of the immortal spirit the old fairy-tale of the stork bringing the baby from the skies has more truth in it than the bald 'factual' answers which children are given today. To make physical birth or physical conception, however much it may be characterised as 'the way in which God works', the origin of the individual ego is the same as to make the physical earth the origin of all consciousness. When Natural Science can answer the question of the origin of consciousness in general, it may also be in a position to explain the origin of the individual conscious ego. At present it cannot pretend to answer the child's question: Where do I come from? It can only describe certain processes necessary to the child's bodily arrival on the earth.

The adolescent is ripe for the discussion of such questions of the origin of life, consciousness and the self-conscious ego; they release the question of sex from its purely physical associations and can be raised quite objectively in the study of History, Literature, Zoology or what you will. But he will probably prove indifferent to the great issues involved if he has been conditioned as a younger child by purely materialistic explanations of what are in reality spiritual events.

There remains, however, the question of the erotic sensations

[3] Chapter XII, p. 129.

and practices which puberty brings and which may only too easily monopolise the child's mind and energy at this age. It is of much importance whether a child experiences puberty more in the soul than in the body, or the reverse. If he has had an artistic education, a rich soul life will take hold of the new element and transform it. It is the intellectualised child—and this does not necessarily mean the clever child—who often has the greatest difficulty at puberty. A great deal therefore depends on a child's earlier education.

It is here that the principle of metamorphosis—to which much allusion has already been made—must especially be taken into consideration. It is a universal love, a love of the world, which is the highest expression of puberty. When the individual first begins to feel himself as an entity apart from the world he is for the first time in a position to love that world. What will best prepare such a love in the child? It is to foster in him the faculty of wonder. In wonder the universe awakens a response of feeling in the child. The small child has not yet the faculty of replying actively to what he receives. But as he achieves greater maturity he can make a response. He can go out to the universe in love in the same measure as he formerly received it in wonder. By such transformations are the ages of childhood linked together, 'bound each to each by natural piety'.

This interplay of ages naturally does not exclude wonder from the age of adolescence itself. The more the adolescent can be brought to wonder at all the new things he will learn, the better it will be. But it will be best of all if he can be brought to wonder at Man himself and echo the words of the great Chorus in the *Antigone*, 'Many are the wonders, and no wonder greater than Man.' This is especially the aim of a most important period of lessons in the History of Art which is given in a Waldorf School at this age and which will be described in the following chapter. Indeed the selection of suitable subjects and their right treatment for the age is a matter of the highest art. On it may well depend whether throughout his life a man will live in a sense of harmony with the world, or whether he will be haunted by some inner frustration and discord. The immediate and sensational incidence of juvenile delinquency is only one of the problems of puberty. It is a critical age for the whole of life.

CHAPTER XVIII

The High School—Ninth Grade

By the time children reach adolescence they are beginning to show marked abilities in one direction or another. It is the age when in our educational system specialisation begins, even if it has not begun earlier. The call for technicians in the modern world results for many children in the virtual abandonment of the humanities in favour of a narrowing group of sciences. On the other hand the children who are gifted in the humanities—especially if they are destined for scholarships—hear little more of the sciences and grow up scientifically illiterate.

It is easy to decry the division, but we must first answer the question whether specialisation does, in fact, accord with the natural course of man's development. Ever since Tubal-cain specialised in working brass and iron, men seem to have developed peculiar faculties spontaneously. It is certainly possible to discover strong bents in children well before adolescence. To a large extent these are to be attributed to heredity, or, perhaps more commonly, to the influence of parents and others on the child's imitative powers. There is, however, an impressive residue of children who develop talents or genius for which no heredity or environment can possibly account. Such individuals overcome those forces to which most people are subdued. Perhaps they are the type of a future humanity.

In the case of real genius pretty well the only course a teacher can take is to see that it is not hampered or hindered, though the laws of life work strongly and it almost seems that genius needs some counterforce against which to battle and struggle. Would the music of Mozart have been nobler if his life had been as easy as Mendelssohn's? or the poetry of Keats richer if he had made a happy marriage? The average teacher is not likely to encounter genius, however. The more general question concerns us here of the child endowed with some strong bent of mind or ability.

If a child has exceptional talent in one direction, it need not necessarily mean that he is defective in others. Even with quite ordinary children, being 'bad at a subject' is very frequently an induced rather than a natural state. Perhaps the child made a bad beginning and was frightened by some initial difficulties: perhaps he disliked his teacher: perhaps his parents or older brother had told him how hard a new subject would be and he approached it with his mind made up for failure. There may even be a certain snobbery in announcing that you are incapable in Mathematics or Latin. The average man, no less than the genius, could often be more of an all-round fellow than he imagines.

In reality it is a desperate need of the age to keep young people's minds open to all facets of life as long as possible. The very form of man is a lesson against premature specialisation. It is the animal which rushes headlong into some special function, running, climbing, burrowing, or swimming, with its appropriate form of body and limb: the man holds back, and preserves a physical structure adapted to none of these things, but capable of them all. He is the least specialised of all the creatures of the earth.

Indeed the more specialised life becomes the more socially important it is for every individual to have a general grasp of what is going on in the world, and the more spiritually urgent it is for him to maintain something of the universality of manhood. Men live on the earth together in order that they may share a common life. Each is created in the image of the universe with universal powers and interests. 'Born a man, died a tailor' is as ignoble an epitaph for a man as 'Born a drone, died a drone' is natural for a bee.

It is in accordance with this general view of life that even in its upper classes a Waldorf School endeavours to maintain as broad an education as possible, and in particular to preserve the co-education of Arts and Sciences. There is therefore a general curriculum for all children, on the basis of which more advanced work can be done concurrently by more gifted pupils. But all children enjoy the social experience of learning about the world together, and thereby helping each other to acquire that universality of view which can alone make man a social being.

In planning such a curriculum it is no less important than in the earlier years that the subjects are related to the child's whole development. That the child shall find in the world something that corresponds to what he is experiencing inwardly—this is an axiom of Waldorf education. Differences of time, place and nation will naturally call for modification, both obvious and subtle, in the subjects chosen and their treatment. Nevertheless the suggestions made by Rudolf Steiner for the upper classes of the first Waldorf School bear the stamp of a whole age upon them, and will for long be taken as the supreme example of a liberal education for adolescents.

The critical spirit of adolescence must first be recalled. The children feel that they have their feet on the earth and they want to live in the modern world. Ostensibly they like to reject all forms of idealism and often take pleasure in expressing the most outrageous opinions. Beneath the surface, however, they are dreadfully unsure of themselves and have a secret longing for an example, a hero who represents the ideal they secretly cherish and on whom they can model their lives. The curriculum therefore has two main functions: to bring the children to a knowledge of the forces which have shaped modern life, and at the same time to foster, in as objective a way as possible, their latent idealism. In doing the former it must not leave out of account the problems which modern life has created: in performing the latter it must strenuously avoid anything which may appear sentimental or unpractical.

It is plain that History in the ninth Grade must deal fundamentally with modern times. The great revolutions in thinking which led to the Newtonian view of a mechanical universe forms an excellent introduction. The way in which the work of one astronomer led to that of another, the sequence of Copernicus, Tycho Brahe, Galileo, Kepler and Newton forms a wonderful example of science crossing the frontiers of nations just at the time when the spirit of nationality was raising its ambivalent head in Europe. The mechanical inventions on the earth are, so to speak, reflections of Newton's mechanical universe—one of the early steam-engines was actually called the Sun and Planet engine. The broad sequence of these inventions and their effect on social life down to modern times is a vital chapter in human history. Not less important—and very welcome to the children's hearts—is the growing sense of the importance of the individual and the 'dignity of man' which happily comes to meet the Industrial Revolution. The development of theories of social contracts and of natural rights, the Civil War in England, the American War of Independence, and the French Revolution—all variously interconnected—spring from that same sense of the absolute value of the individual first taught by the Christian Church, but only realised in the social sphere when man came to be master of the physical forces of the earth. The conquest of the earth itself, the opening up of America, Africa and Asia to the white man is an external picture of what the adolescent is feeling in himself. He too has conquered the earth and mastered its powers.

The Science teaching should naturally supplement and enrich the History. At this age the question children ask of the inventions of man is *How* rather than *What*. It is a usual choice in the Waldorf School to answer this *How* first of all in the two fields of the Heat Engine and the Telephone.

There are a variety of reasons for this choice. Historically these are the two inventions which, for good or ill, began the process of making a unity of this diverse world, and our dependence on them (and their progeny) is still immense. The knowledge of how they work is, therefore, not merely of technical interest but of the greatest social importance. If you use a telephone or travel by train without knowing the mechanical and technical processes involved you cannot relate yourself in thought to the people who are serving you. However social your nature, you have erected a barrier between you and them. Not that you should always be talking to technicians about their subjects, but the fact that you understand broadly what their job involves makes an invisible bond between you and them.

There is, however, a still deeper reason for this choice of subject. It is now generally recognised that the simple tools man uses are nothing more than an extension of his hand. The animal has commonly developed the hand into one particular tool. He is expert with his one tool, but can use no other. The human hand can do many things, it can burrow and shovel and throw; it is a hammer, a pair of pincers, or a wrench; but all in a primitive way. Man has invented tools to carry further the natural capacity of his hands.

What applies to the hand however is true in a subtler way for other parts of the human organism as well. Almost all machines are mechanical externalisations of some principle in man. It is far less true to regard processes in man as mechanical than to look on machines as copies at a lower level of life processes in man. A bellows mimics a lung: but a lung is not a bellows. The process of converting heat into energy was established in the metabolism of man long before it was copied in the heat machine. The nervous system was a living vehicle of consciousness ages in advance of its mechanical counterpart in telephone and telegraph.

The fitness of these two studies of heat engine and telephone at this age lies in the fact, already enlarged upon, that adolescents are living especially strongly in the two opposite systems of the head and nerves on the one hand and the metabolism and limbs on the other: to put it more exactly, the process of growth has reached the limbs and the process of awakening has penetrated to the head. Hence arise the two poles of adolescence—the cold cutting criticism on the one hand and the flaming indignation (and other passions) on the other. For the time being the rhythmical life is overwhelmed by these two extremes and the adolescent finds it hard to preserve his balance.

One of the ways of helping children at this stage, therefore, is to externalise their difficulties. It is not without significance that the rise of the heat engine coincides with the fall of the great age of human passions. The Victorian Englishmen who developed the first railways were very different in character from the great explorers of the Elizabethan age. Not a few of them actually followed the 'Quaker rule that doth the human feeling cool'. The inventions of man are the complement of his inner struggles and conquests.

There is therefore good reason why the scientific teaching at this age stresses two inventions so closely related to the adolescent's own development. It is in such special cases that the difference of treatment between the Class teacher and the specialist can clearly be seen. The former will have covered the story of heat engines in a general descriptive way from Newcomen's atmospheric pump to the locomotive (still so important in all parts of the world), the turbine and the internal combustion engine. He will have given short biographies of the principal inventors and discussed the general principles involved. In the ninth class, however, the heat engine must be treated quite scientifically. Technical drawings will be made, the laws of pressure and expansion will be studied and practical problems worked out. The children should be astonished to discover how much there is to learn about things which they have perhaps come to look on as already familiar.

Bernard Shaw once said that the young generation ought to be given long and detailed lessons on the working of the motor-car and strictly forbidden any acquaintance with the arts. Young people would then, he thought, develop a clandestine passion for poetry, music and painting, and grow up into civilised men and women. It is certainly true that technically minded children will more readily pay attention to artistic subjects if their mechanical interests are first satisfied. Even at the comparatively philistine age of puberty children can be made aware of the unique place which art occupies in human life if the right way is found to do so. There is no better subject for awakening the first idealism of youth than a study of the visual arts.

It has been said that in two spheres of activity man encounters a rigid necessity. In thinking he is bound by the laws of logic: in his practical creations he is equally constrained by physical and mechanical laws. In art he creates freely—and yet finds in the end that he has himself made a new law within the sphere of that creation. It is the place in which the Creature most nearly reaches the part of the Creator.

The origin of art is lost in obscurity. All that archaeologists can tell us is that even among the earliest artifacts of man there are many on which care seems to have been spent to make them beautiful as well as useful. Paintings and musical pipes are among his earliest productions. Whatever the purpose of Palaeolithic cave paintings, in execution they must rank as astonishing works of art, and would seem alone to verify Chesterton's dictum that almost the only thing we know about primitive man is that he was not primitive.

Nowhere does man reveal his inner life and his ideals so objectively as in his visible works of art. In the development of art from Egypt and Chaldaea to Greece and Rome we see the transition from a theocratic to a human society. In contrasts with Classical art the pictures and sculptures of the Middle Ages show an inwardness of feeling and depth of soul which the Hellenic sculptors never imagined or attempted to portray. In the transition from Cimabue and Giotto to the great Dutch and Flemish masters religious art becomes secular. First there is the Saint or the Virgin with the gold background which shines with the spiritual light of the world. Then an earthly landscape—though often the scene of a religious story, the flight into Egypt or the Three Kings coming over the hills—supplants the heavenly gold. At last only the landscape remains: or the interior, no longer the scene of the Annunciation, but of a music lesson or a girl reading a letter.

All this development of mankind, so plainly seen in his works of art, is of immense importance to the adolescent. It shows him humanity growing 'ripe for the earth' as he is growing ripe himself. But it also raises in an objective way questions of past and future ideals stimulating and strengthening to his dawning inner life.

The wonderfully faithful colouring of modern transparencies make it possible for children today to be ennobled by great paintings as never before.[1] It is easier for children at this age to express what they feel about the visual arts than about music or poetry. It is a matter of experience in Waldorf Schools that it is by no means the more intellectually gifted children who will say the most profound things about the picture at which the class has been gazing. His very quickness often prevents the intellectual from dwelling with sufficient devotion on the object contemplated. The slower child can show him how to forget himself in pondering on a Giotto or a Leonardo or a Rembrandt.

What can or should be done in English literature at this age will depend immensely on how the children have been taught before. It is a common complaint among teachers at University level that students come to them without any real sense of rhythm. But if this sense has been kept alive by good teaching, it is just in rhythm that a first beginning can be made in the conscious aesthetic appreciation of poetry. In what a wonderful variety of rhythms and rhyme schemes poems are written! Either in contrasting poems, or in those where there is a constant change of rhythm, such as Tennyson's *Revenge* or Chesterton's *Lepanto*, children can discover the fitness both of the general rhythm and of the rhythm of each line. Many of them will wish to experiment with rhythms of their own. It is important always to expatiate on what is good rather than criticise what is bad. Young people will only too easily catch the pernicious habit of 'debunking'.

This more intimate kind of criticism will be taken much

[1] A specially fine collection has been made by the Art Master of Michael Hall, a Rudolf Steiner School in England, who has himself photographed throughout Europe and America.

further in the tenth Grade when the children are more mature. Literature has a special gift to offer children of the earlier age—the gift of drama, and especially of comedy. A character like Falstaff, so much of the world, with such a gift for making the most of any situation, so full of surprises, witty himself and the cause of wit in others, appeals immensely to the child's growing sense of personality. So do the splendid heroics of Prince Hal when he becomes Henry V. Indeed these historical plays of Shakespeare contain all the elements the young adolescent needs. He is not yet ready for the more romantic plays or for the deeper tragedies. The intellectual subtleties of the eighteenth century also elude him. Among the Romantic poets he will appreciate Byron more than Wordsworth or Shelley. For Byron has something of the Elizabethan in him in his passionate craving for excitement and the fullness of life. With Scott (whom he superseded in this respect) Byron is the last representative of an age when it was thought natural to prefer a romantic tale in verse to one in prose. After his first great success as a verse writer Scott published his early prose tales anonymously for fear of losing his reputation. It is an age which can be recaptured in the adolescent, who will listen eagerly to a robust verse tale when read aloud to him. It is no small achievement if young people come to take rhythm for granted as a vehicle for telling a story.

There is one task in the teaching of literature which is more important today than ever before—encouraging children to read for themselves—to which reference has already been made. The History teacher can do much in this respect at this age for he is covering the period in which good historical novels abound, and he can show the children how much they can learn about the 'flavour' of a period as well as of its actual events from selected novels and biographies.

The all too prevalent habit of asking children to write a 'book report' on the books they have read is of doubtful value. The book report is generally a brief précis of the contents with a few personal remarks of pleasure or displeasure at the end. There are certain kinds of documents which properly call for précis, an art which children should learn in its right context. Novels are emphatically not in this class, and biographies only if they are bad. It is far better to ask the children to use their imagination in carrying the book further, or developing a scene the author has left undescribed. If the author has described a scene in the summer, can they describe it in the winter? What will the young hero be like as an old man? What did the Wedding Guest in the *Ancient Mariner* tell his friends as they came home from the wedding? The art of writing is to persuade the reader to enter into the world described with all his powers. Anything the teacher asks the children to do should take them further into the mood, scene and characters of the book. To criticise and condense is to withdraw.

One other subject is necessary to give a general picture of the ninth Grade curriculum. In Mathematics is to be found the greatest certainty of thinking. A mathematical or geometrical proof is entirely self-sustaining. It is therefore a salutary thing, just when the adolescent's powers of thought are awakening, to give him confidence in the validity of thinking. But it befits his age that this should be in a practical sphere which he can easily envisage. For this purpose the mathematics of chance and permutations and combinations are excellent. The children discover to their surprise that thinking can easily solve problems which seem at first sight too complex to admit of any solution. Nor is this process difficult —even the least mathematical children rejoice to find that their thinking enables them to achieve the impossible. This leads to some study of irrational numbers, for example $\sqrt{2}$ which is of great importance in all mensuration, the diagonal of the square being its side multiplied by $\sqrt{2}$. Geometry also advances to the study of regular solids. For the children should grasp in geometrical thought also the three dimensional earth which they are inheriting.

This leads, finally, to the subject of Geography. It is a grasp of the whole earth which should be sought at this age. The great mountain ranges, which are like the bones of the earth, should especially be studied, the East–West direction of the ranges of Europe and Asia uniting with the North–South line of the American mountains to form something like a great cross on the surface of the entire earth. But at the same time some special nexus of mountains—such as the Alps or the Rockies—should be taken for special study. The children should know which are the oldest of the earth's mountains, and which have appeared at a comparatively recent date.

When Francis Bacon wrote his essay on what he thought a

garden should be he described it as the 'platform of a garden'. It is a good word because it embodies several notions, something to be copied, something elevated to which one may aspire, but at the same time something of a foundation on which new things may be built. Rudolf Steiner's curriculum for a modern High School is such a 'platform'. The ninth Grade (which is the first High School Grade) is specially important, not only because it gives the foundation for the three subsequent Grades, but because it is the critical age for puberty. The following year brings a new measure of self-confidence and balance. It will bring it to the extent to which the ninth Grade has richly prepared the ground.

CHAPTER XIX

The High School—Tenth Grade

It is interesting to see the lively and original way in which the Waldorf curriculum for the tenth Grade sets out to meet the development of this age. Naturally the co-education of the arts and sciences is continued, but it is in the sphere of the arts that the advance is most revolutionary, especially in the subject of History.

In the ninth Grade the children have become immersed in modern times. In the tenth they are transplanted to the ancient world, and study the whole field of the old civilisations up to the culmination of Hellenic culture, when for the first time the West flowed back upon the East in the conquests of Alexander the Great. It is a startling transition but there are many reasons which justify its choice.

In the Renaissance the classical Graeco-Roman culture woke to a new and transformed life. The Classics took the place of the old *Trivium* in the Schools of Europe, the study of Greek was revived, and works of Graeco-Roman art sprang like magic from their graves in Italian soil. Modern man has witnessed something like a second Renaissance. Old civilisations have given themselves up to his spade, and his detective genius has reconstructed the exterior of their life. In art and architecture their influence has been immense. But the forms of their civilisation also have been repeated—for good or ill—in ours. For the first time since the old River civilisations we are witnessing economies based on irrigation: their forcible transplanting of whole peoples has been repeated in our day; the mass organisation and the planned city, the conquest of foreign lands for raw materials—all these were practised thousands of years ago on the Nile and the Euphrates. It is as natural, and as important, for modern children to learn about Egypt or Babylon or the Aztecs as it was natural for the Renaissance child to learn about Athens or Rome. Ancient History may fairly be said to be the most modern there is.

Moreover there is a special reason for the transition to ancient history just at this time. Many young people today are completely imprisoned in the limitations of the age. Nothing could be better for them, while their minds are still plastic, than to be brought face to face with a world of values so different from their own. For it goes without saying that every endeavour must be made to enter with the greatest sympathy into what appear to modern consciousness the strangest customs. For instance, we must not scorn the practice of embalming the dead or burying them with the appurtenances of life, nor laugh at the Egyptian representations of animal-headed Gods. If we think that a people who believed in the moral judgment of the soul after death, and who knew a great deal about anatomy, imagined that the mummied body was actually going to eat the food provided, sail in the model boat and ride in the model chariot, then we are more naïve than we imagine the Egyptians to have been.

The difficulty of men in ancient times was to come to terms with the physical world. Modern man experiences the opposite difficulty—he is so imprisoned in the physical that he can hardly conceive the existence of a spiritual world. But at the dawn of civilisation man needed potent aids to bring him down to the earth. Some individuals even in later times have experienced a similar need. The poet Wordsworth records that when he was a boy in the beautiful English Lake District he sometimes felt himself so transported into the heavens that on his way to school he had to hold on to a gate to keep himself on earth. The Pyramids, the Ziggurats, the Megalithic Monuments are the gates by which man held himself to the earth. But the preservation of the body with the articles familiar in life was intended to prolong after death the memory and experience of the earth. Other civilisations which had not this end in view, burned or exposed their dead. The artificial preservation of the bodily form was a new stage in human experience.

Another most important characteristic of the ancient world difficult for modern thought to realise is that the human mind then worked not with ideas but with pictures. Sometimes it was even necessary to enact the picture, and bring it directly into the sphere of the will. When the prophet Ahijah wanted to tell Jeroboam that he would become king of ten of the twelve tribes of Israel, he pulled off Jeroboam's new garment, tore it into twelve pieces and gave him ten! Even apart from such drastic action, thoughts naturally appeared as pictures. Rehoboam's little finger was thicker than his father's loins; Solomon chastised his people with whips, he would chastise them with scorpions. But it is in their relation to dreams that we see most characteristically the difference between the ancient and the modern mind. The Pharaoh's dream, interpreted by Joseph, regulates the economy of all Egypt: Gilgamesh cannot govern Erech aright till he finds the man of nature, Enkidu, who dreams for him. It was the order of life that the young men should see visions, and the old men should dream dreams.

It was the Hellenes who transformed picture-consciousness into intellectual consciousness. They were the first to examine life with the power of thought, not excluding from that examination the life of thought itself. We can see the transformation in the course of their history. The vision of the Furies became the invisible sting of conscience; the revelation of Athene giving the thoughts to man became first the impersonal 'It thinks in me' and then the entirely self-conscious 'I think': the pictures of the oracles—no longer self-sufficient—had first to be interpreted into idea, and then disappeared altogether.

The transformation culminated in the thought of Aristotle which dominated the West for two millenniums after Alexander had spread it from India to Egypt.

In following this period of history, therefore, the children are witnessing that birth of thinking which is taking place in them, and which their own thinking is now sufficiently mature to realise. Nearly all modern problems came to light with astonishing clarity in the history of Greece—social, political, economic and scientific. There is no better foundation for understanding almost any subject than the School of Hellas. But the School of Hellas is not autochthonous. It is born out of the picture-wisdom which was the wisdom of the East.

Rudolf Steiner's indications for the right kind of course in literature are no less interesting, though in literature those indications must naturally be translated afresh into the idiom of the country. In a different sphere the literature lessons are intended to show the same fundamental development as appears in the teaching of History. The Hellenes experienced the birth of the self-conscious ego principally in the sphere of thinking; the peoples of northern Europe more in the sphere of the will. Thus for German children Steiner suggested a study of the medieval

Nibelungenlied (which includes an introduction to older forms of the German language) and its comparison with the *Edda,* the same story in its more ancient form. The consciousness of the later age has completely transformed the story. The descent of Wotan to the earth 'one-eyed and seeming ancient', the planting of the sword in the Branstock, the gold of Fafnir are almost entirely forgotten and we see a world of feudal obligations and courtly ceremonial. Above all other changes is the change in love and loyalty. In the *Edda* you live by the blood tie, you are faithful to your brothers and treacherous to your husband; in the *Nibelungenlied* you are treacherous to your brothers and faithful to your husband. Romantic love is born. The *Nibelungenlied* contains what is perhaps the first historical description of the act of falling in love.

The story of Odin and Sigurd-Fafnir's-bane was no doubt as familiar to the Anglo-Saxons as to any other people of Germanic stock. But it was entirely superseded first by Christian lore and then by classical mythology and had to be recovered again in the nineteenth century. From Chaucer onwards English literature is steeped in classical mythology. The English imagination has therefore been enriched from two sources, Northern and Southern. We may therefore prefer (if a choice must be made) to take a similar example of development from a more ancient field.

It has been recorded that when certain Greeks were once in India they saw some plays acted in the villages, as they are acted to this day, and believed they were seeing a dramatic representation of the *Iliad.* What they were actually witnessing, however, was undoubtedly a performance of scenes from the old Indian epic the *Mahabharrata,* in which the culminating fight between the two champions, Arjuna and Karna, might well be taken for the duel between Hector and Achilles. In fact, however, the older Eastern epic differs from the Western in the same way as the *Edda* differs from the *Nibelungenlied.* In the Indian story the hero is Arjuna who is never represented alone but always in the company of his mother and his four Pandu brothers. His adversary, Karna, whom he defeats, is the lonely individual without family or country. In the Greek epic Hector is the man shown to us in all his connections of family and race, but he is overcome by the lonely and homeless Achilles, who has cut himself off from all his fellow Greeks to nurse his anger in his tent. That is, all except one. For Achilles is one of those individuals, of whom several are shown us in ancient literature, who represent something new in the world—the principle of friendship. David and Jonathan, Orestes and Pylades, Achilles and Patroclus, Gilgamesh and Enkidu, these are the types of the new impulse which was to sweep away the old blood tie. Achilles fights not for his family but to revenge the death of his friend.

Similar contrasts may be found in comparing the treatment of a theme by a classical and a modern author. In Aeschylus' play, Prometheus has to be released by an external agent: in Shelley's *Prometheus Unbound* the Titan undergoes an inner evolution: it is when he has overcome all thoughts of anger and revenge, and wishes 'no living thing to suffer pain' that the chains drop from him of their inevitable accord. Or perhaps an example may be sought in Shakespeare, who is the greatest educator that young people can ever meet. They are mature enough now for such a play as *Romeo and Juliet*—where Shakespeare is handling that theme of the blood feud so dear to ancient dramatists. But in the ancient world a blood feud can only be ended by external purification or the intervention of a god. It is the impulse of love and of sacrifice which in Shakespeare ends the long feuds of the Montagues and Capulets.

All this must be taken as suggestion. It is the theme which matters, not the variations. But some at least of the works selected must be studied in detail. The children should begin to know what thorough knowledge means. It will almost certainly be found advisable to act part at least of a play each succeeding year. Nothing unites so many divergent talents, nothing gives so deep an experience of literature, nothing is so truly educational as the acting of a play. It is a liberal education in itself to be immersed in a production of some great drama.

It will have been observed how admirably the main theme of literature complements the chosen period of history. The same can be said of a special period devoted during the year to the study of what may be called the art of literature. The children can now begin to be conscious of all that made them love poetry instinctively when they were younger: rhythm, imagery, the ring of words, the joy in a tale. To take the first alone, which can now be developed much further than in the preceding year, what a wonderful variety of rhythms have been invented by man. How impossible it is to reproduce the rhythm of one age or country in another. The hexameter has one quality—and Matthew Arnold's *Essay on Translating Homer* admirably demonstrates that no other metre has the same qualities. The alliterative metre of the Northern epics—Beowulf and the like—is a rock-obstructed torrent compared with the broad flow of the stately Greek river. How different, too, is the imagery of North and South: the Greek delighting in long similes where the original is almost forgotten in the detail of the comparison, the Northern epic abounding in incisive picture-words, swanway for river, breast-hoard for thoughts, whale-road for sea. The children will find in the forms of literature something of the same difference they saw the previous year between Northern and Southern paintings. There is much of the Greek quality of harmonious perfection in Raphael or Leonardo: much of the starkness and wilfulness of the North in Dürer and Grünewald.

These are comparatively external and tangible differences and can be a prelude to others of a more subtle kind. There is the difference between blank verse and rhyme, between prose and poetry, between rhymed stanzas and the continuous flow of couplets, between one lyric form and another—and the amazing difference in the same form as used by different writers.

The last difference will naturally lead into a deeper and more extensive acquaintance with the Romantic poets than was possible in the previous year. There is something of a temperamental difference to be observed in this group of poets: Shelley the lover of ever-changing images, sanguine even in his melancholy: Wordsworth with his melancholic mindfulness of the past: Coleridge choleric in thought but able to bring so little to its final form: Keats with that promise of the union of all virtues which is perhaps only to be found elsewhere in Shakespeare. They will appeal to different children. Nor must the modern writers be forgotten. The adolescent likes to feel he is up to date. Indeed it may even be advisable to introduce the older poets via the modern. It is not a history of literature which is required at this time, but the making conscious of an experience.

The Science curriculum is basically concerned with the earth and the substances which compose it. In this it is really founded on the teaching of geography, which, as in the ninth Grade, is again concerned with the whole of the earth. The former Grade dealt especially with the mountain formations: this can now be extended to climate, vegetation, the distribution of animals and the characteristic races of mankind. Geography is a subject which may be said to embrace almost all other subjects, and must be limited by emphasis rather than by boundaries. The emphasis for this Grade is on the rocks and soils and how (together with climate) they affect all forms of life. It leads directly into chemistry.

For in Chemistry the central theme is the mutual interrelation of salt, acid and base, as it appears in the substances of the earth and in man himself. It is good to make a beginning with limestone. When limestone is heated it separates into quicklime and carbonic acid gas. There is a complete polarity between these two constituents. The former is solid, the latter volatile. The one becomes alkaline when mingled with water: it deadens the taste and lowers consciousness: it turns litmus blue and appears in the head of man and in the roots of plants. The other becomes acid when mingled with water: it stings the tongue and raises consciousness: it turns litmus red and is found in the fruit of plants and in the digestive organs of man. The same polarity can be equally well produced by burning a simple substance such as straw, when the fumes will be acid and the ash alkaline.

The important thing, however, is to bring the same process to light in the human organism as well. It is the process of breathing which is the equivalent in man to this fire process outside. The fire-breathing dragon is an externalised picture of what is a more intimate process in man! When we breathe we burn oxygen, and the burning brings about a double process: we exhale acid air, and deposit an alkaline substance, which appears in our bones.

It is in the limestone hill or mountain, formed by organic combustion, whose many fossils bear witness to its origin, that we find the rounded form characteristic of our bones. The silicate mountains, which bear no fossils and have a quite different origin, form sharp and defined forms, peaks and spires and spikes. Silica appears in man in the delicate substance of the hair, and in birds in the fine forms of the feathers. And the stream tumbles off silica mountains in cataracts and torrents, like water off a duck's back: while the limestone mountains suck the water into secret underground caverns, like the marrow within the bone.

Limestone is soluble in acid, silica in alkali. The alumina—clay and slate soils—are soluble in both. Thus we find the three great soils of the earth form a polarity with a middle term. Nor must it be forgotten that the discovery of the chemistry of these three substances is fundamental to the civilisation of man. Quicklime for building, clay for pottery, silica for glass—these, together with the use of the far rarer metals, were the earliest and perhaps remain still the most evolutionary of all the chemical discoveries of man.

Much more could be added but the intention is only to indicate the way in which some characteristic thoughts find their realisation in different fields of life, and thus unite them together. It is an axiom of chemistry that no chemical combinations can take place without the presence of water. Fire separates, water combines. The salt, separated into base and acid by fire, is re-created as salt again when the two meet in water. Man's enthusiasm and determination has separated knowledge into various 'subjects'. But behind the subjects stand the great unifying thoughts and principles whose function, like that of water, is to combine. To develop these thoughts in any given field would require a book—and a specialist—for each subject. But it is when the specialists share common thoughts and a common philosophy that the impact of their teaching is most salutary. The adolescent is uncertain and divided within himself. All the more does he need a unifying influence from without.

Finally, a word must be said about the mathematical sciences. Mathematical ability is exceptional in that it matures early. It has been remarked that great mathematicians have commonly made their significant contribution to the science before the age of thirty. The difference in mathematical ability will therefore probably be more marked in adolescence than in the case of other subjects. It is for this reason that mathematics are often virtually abandoned at this age, except for the more able pupils. It is surprising with how little mathematics a man can get successfully through life, even in a mathematical age.

There is a great danger in this policy. The mathematical physicists are becoming a new pontificate. They share a private, almost occult, knowledge from which they produce not only their revolutionary inventions, but their still more revolutionary views on the nature of matter and of life. It is important therefore that as many people as possible shall possess at least enough mathematical knowledge to understand what the mathematical physicist is doing, both in the atomic sphere and in that of the solid state. There is perhaps no subject which has such value as mathematics at the two opposite poles of intrinsic theoretical content, and practical application in life.

The mathematical curriculum in a Waldorf School therefore enters realms which are not commonly opened in schools, as well as teaching the subject from a different point of view. Arithmetic, for instance, advances to a study of transcendental numbers. Trigonometry begins from the circle and from the problem of determining π, starting with the Archimedean calculation of its value. Logarithms are introduced, but their function in describing growth forces in nature is stressed. For the logarithm appears in the growth of algae, in the culture of bacilli, in the spiral of the shell-fish, in the cochlea of the ear, and so on. But in logarithmic growth the basis is not the number 10, commonly taken for practical purpose, but the transcendental number e. In such a number we see the working in nature of something not expressible in earthly terms. It is as though something of the infinite entered the sphere of the finite earth.

Geometry, similarly, is principally concerned with conic curves, which can be developed in a variety of ways. But one special study is the transformation of form from the ellipse through the parabola to the hyperbola. The ellipse has two foci in finite space and therefore encloses a finite area. But if one of the foci is moved along the axis to infinity, the resulting curve is a parabola. If the movement is continued so that the moving focus returns from infinity from the opposite direction, a third curve arises, the hyperbola, which appears to be in two parts but is geometrically one, the hands of its two pairs of arms clasped together, as it were at infinity. It therefore encloses, not a finite, but an infinite area.

Such a possibility of passing in thought from the finite to the infinite is of great value to the mind of the adolescent. The 'shades of the prison house' are closing heavily upon him, and he is in danger of losing for ever the Heaven which lay about him in his infancy. To be able to use this new weapon of thought to cut through the walls of this prison, to think in terms of the infinite, and yet relate the infinite to the spatial and the visible, is like a kind of spiritual breathing. Thought begins to find its way back to its spiritual origins.

It is one of the tragedies of materialism that it does not understand even the earthly. To understand the physical through the spiritual is the goal to which the human mind must aspire. The adolescent with his dawning thought can also glimpse the distant heights.

CHAPTER XX

The High School—Eleventh and Twelfth Grades

In the eleventh and twelfth Grades the present conditions of entry into university, college or profession makes specialisation in most countries inevitable. A Waldorf School, however, endeavours to preserve a generous measure of general education as the soil from which the special subjects can grow. It is only such a general education that can meet and satisfy the peculiar needs of their maturing age. Specialised studies take their form and content not in relation to the student but from their subject-matter alone.

It is particularly unfortunate if young people at this age become unduly specialised. For the modern specialist, in the sciences above all, is principally concerned with the question *How*. Natural Science (at its best) does not pretend to tell us what electricity or light or gravity are, or what they mean: it only tells us how they work. Even the specialist in the humanities has admitted more and more of the scientific 'how' into his studies. This question of 'how' is that in which the younger adolescent is principally interested. But as he grows older, he invariably begins to ask himself another question: What is this world, and what am I that I am placed within it? Generally his education continues only to answer *How,* when he has begun to ask *What*?

It is therefore not only a question of giving a comprehensive picture of the world to conclude the child's school life, important as this is. He must at least glimpse the possibility of understanding what the world is. That understanding may not go very far at this age. But unless the curtain is parted a little at the critical time, it will only too easily densify into an iron one, and the adult will go through life believing that the ultimate questions are unanswerable, or falling back on a faith which his conscious mind and his reason cannot support or justify.

Once again, in a general work only a few indications can be given of the kind of educational experience for which a Waldorf School strives. The core of the matter will perhaps best appear in one principal approach to history and literature.

The historical age with which the modern mind generally finds it most difficult to come to terms is the age of the gradual penetration of Christianity into the Western world. We understand (or think we understand) the arguments of Socrates and the Platonic doctrine of ideas; but we are baffled by the Church Fathers whose acrimonious disputations on doctrine appear to us profoundly unreal. We appreciate the Roman ideal of *mens sana in corpore sano*; we are repelled by the austerities and mortifications of the hermits and anchorites. The disappearance of a rational society with great public works and an organised system of government before the rise of a religion credulous of miracles and riddled with superstitions still seems to the intellectual Western mind (as it seemed to Gibbon) a deplorable spectacle.

It is, however, a period unique in all history. For it is the period in which entirely new impulses are taking hold of humanity, arising from that event which in Rudolf Steiner's philosophy is central to all history. In no narrow or dogmatic sense, but as an event fostered and foreseen by all the great religions of the world, he saw the incarnation of the Christ, the *Logos*, the Word, not as a new ethical teaching but as a deed affecting every individual soul no less than the whole course of history. The ferment of the early Christian centuries is a ferment of life in an age whose forms of thought and impulses of will (as Professor Toynbee has pointed out) were too dead to grapple with the social and spiritual problems which the spread of the Roman Empire had aroused. Even externally it is a time of transformation. The organising power of a great Empire becomes that of a great Church. In the days of the Roman Republic mighty generals marched out of the gates of Rome to meet the invading Gaul or German pouring over the passes of the Alps. It was a Pope, clad in the vestments of spiritual power, who stayed the march of Attila and mitigated the plunder of the Vandals. The gladiator disappears, whose only justification was that he taught the Roman youth how to die for his country. He emerges transformed as the Knight, dedicated to the cause of his King, his lady or his religion. The child (once exposed to death at the will of his father) becomes the venerated image of God himself. For the secret of the age is that the Outer has become the Inner, the Word has become Flesh.

Even in its outer manifestations life tries to express an inwardly realised ideal. The separation of the spiritual arm from the secular, the daily miracle of transubstantiation, the organisations for the contemplative and religious life, the mutual loyalties with their spiritual sanctions which lay behind the feudal system, the vows of knighthood—there is nothing like this penetration of spiritual ideals into common practice in the older civilisations. It is no longer a question of external ceremonies, of which there was no lack in paganism, but of a formative principle working from within. The working of this inner formative principle came to its highest expression in transubstantiation, without which early Christendom is unthinkable. When the belief in transubstantiation went, a civilisation went with it.

All this alone would make this period of history a wonderful study for opening in a dispassionate manner those questions concerning the nature of the world and the meaning of life which begin to stir in young people's hearts and minds at this age.

But there is more than this. Alongside the outer development of the Church in its characteristic Roman forms there goes a deeper, more spiritual stream of the Christian impulse which shows itself in legend and poetry and song. Among all the creations of the human mind there is nothing so drenched with spiritual light, so founded on what may be called 'inwardness', as the legends of Arthur and of the Holy Grail. It is to these last in particular that the attention of children is turned in the eleventh Grade.

It may indeed be said that all this cycle of legends gives a picture of transubstantiation of a far wider scope than the transubstantiation (at that time universally credited) in the ceremony of the Mass. The round table is round because it is a model of the heavens, and its company of knights are an earthly society become a heavenly one. Sir Gareth, the kitchen knight, transforms the anger which the taunts of his lady, Lynette, raise in him, into valour against her enemies. But more than that: he begins as the scullion who feeds the coals into the oven, and his nickname of Beau-mains is derisory of his blackened hands: then, when he is granted an adventure, he overcomes first a black knight, then a green, then a red, then a blue; and finally his own armour takes on all colours in turn, till it shines like pure crystal. This is a tale of alchemy. The black carbon passes through the sphere of the colours and becomes the transparent diamond, as the knight enriches and spiritualises his soul. For the true alchemist, as C. G. Jung has demonstrated,[1] was concerned with a moral transformation as an essential condition and corollary of the transformation of substance.

Above all, the knight of the Grail was seeking for such a transformation in order to partake immediately of that spiritual power of which even the host in the Mass could only be a living emblem. It is interesting to see through what qualities different knights in the tradition of different countries achieve, or endeavour to achieve, the Grail: Launcelot, the knight of courage and will, but also of tragic failure in deed; Sir Gawaine with his courtesy and gentleness; Sir Perceval who has to learn to ask the question and tread the road of consciousness; Sir Galahad whose integrity keeps him erect where his father Launcelot had stumbled. There are many spiritual roads to the Grail, but it is the goal of all the knights to achieve a new communion based on no given society—not even on a Round Table—but won through the loneliness of individual striving. We catch a first glimpse of that ultimate society which shall be built entirely on the freedom of the individuals who compose it. There is no depth of interpretation of which such profound legends are not capable.

But these legends should not be left floating in some remote sea of consciousness like an island in a Chinese picture. For instance, the relation of man to substance is the basic study of all economics. How shall the substances of the earth be distributed among mankind, and according to what conception of man and matter? The economic aims and ideals of different societies are the reflection of their thought—or lack of thought—on these questions. The financial organisation of the Templars shows one view of man and the world: the *laissez-faire* of the nineteenth century another: the Socialist belief in public ownership a third. Adam Smith held that in moral questions man is naturally and properly altruistic: in economic matters, equally naturally and properly, he pursues his own self-interest. Are there spheres of society today in which different principles reign, comparable to the spiritual and secular spheres of the Middle Ages? And if so, what is their relation to the life of the individual man?

The young person inwardly longs to see society as a reflection

[1] *Psychology and Alchemy.*

of his ideals; or at least as a potential reflection. It is therefore important to open social and economic questions, not as an isolated field but on the ground of the highest expression of the human spirit. Man is today responsible both for his neighbour and for the earth in a way he has never been responsible before. The youth not only needs, he longs to be aware of this responsibility.

Apart from this tremendous theme, indeed as a corollary to it, the children can now appreciate aspects of their native literature and history which were beyond them before. On the one hand they will be fascinated by the polished epigrammatic style of the eighteenth century which will give them a taste of the elegance of that aristocratic age. On the other, they will understand the depth of the Romantic revolt against this formalism, and the passionate way in which the Romantic poets sought for the spirit in man and in nature. But there should be a background of European experience to this. Shakespeare—and the children can now begin to respond to the great central plays, *Hamlet* or *King Lear* or *Macbeth*—can be compared with the French or Greek dramatists. Milton, whose *Paradise Lost* stands at the beginning of a new age, but is rooted so deeply in the old, can be contrasted with Dante. The English Romantic movement and the American Transcendentalists are hardly to be understood without reference to the German romantics, especially the towering genius of Goethe. In this there should be close co-operation with the teachers of foreign languages in whose lessons the children are now reading some of the great works of foreign literature, and perhaps acting parts of *Faust* or a play of Molière.

With this goes a special study of the development of the most inward of the arts—music. Nothing is more remarkable in modern times than the flowering of musical genius, which perhaps distinguishes the age as much as the development of natural science. Indeed the spiritual striving of mankind now comes to its most potent expression in musical experience. The children's acquaintance with music should now acquire a historical and aesthetic background.

The twelfth Grade should also introduce such writers as Tolstoy, Dostoievski, and Ibsen, who have had so profound an influence on the West. The Russian novelists are in striking contrast with the great English nineteenth-century writers, Dickens,

Thackeray, Hardy, Meredith. The inner struggles and tormented spiritual lives of the characters in the Russian novels have really no counterpart in the English. How different again is the world of Victor Hugo. The character of a people is lucidly presented in their novels. By contrast and comparison of different nations we come to appreciate what infinite variety and untold riches lie in the nature of man. All the wonder which the young children felt for the world should be equalled by the wonder they feel for man. Once again we return to the saying 'Many the wonders, and no wonder greater than Man.'

By this time those children who are more interested in literature will probably have formed clubs, and will be inviting contributions from outsiders, as well as teachers, on various subjects, and no doubt often on the most modern authors. Not every child will develop his interest so far, but the key to the kingdom of literature can be put in the hands of all. It will be necessary to be drastically selective, but the aim will be through concrete examples to open a vision and stimulate an interest which will grow with advancing years.

For historical studies, if it has been possible to cover the development of the early Christian centuries and the Middle Ages in the eleventh class, the twelfth should be devoted mainly to a revision and review of history in general. This should not be so much a chronological review as an examination of history in the search for the answer to some fundamental questions. The question of whether there is form and meaning in history at all can be raised in connection with older and modern philosophers. The children should know, for instance, the organic theory of the life of civilisation propounded by Spengler: and the modern views of Toynbee based on the process of challenge and response. Is there development only within a given civilisation? Or does humanity progress from one civilisation to another, even if there is no direct influence to be discerned? Some civilisations, like the Greek, seem to have a beginning (the Homeric age), a middle (the age of Pericles) and an end (the time of Alexander and Aristotle): others, like the Chinese, have never come to an end: the American had no beginning. What do such differences mean? In the light of such questions, by contrast and comparison, the whole of history can be reviewed.

There was a time when men could live within the history of

their own country and people, though it has always been against the best educational traditions of the West to do so. But that time has gone. Not only has the Ganges flowed into the Thames, the Yellow River has flowed into the Potomac, the Rhine into the Mississippi, and the Seven Seas have become one sea. The remotest past and the insistent future are rushing together in the present with a force never before known. Every man has his roots in the whole earth, and the winds of the entire world play through the branches of his mind.

* * *

The picture of science teaching in these last two classes of a Waldorf School is even more difficult to describe than that of the humanities. It may very briefly be said to have two objects: to give a clear account of the achievements (and limitations) of modern science; and to show the possibilities of other approaches to the world of phenomena which might give other pictures of the universe. Rudolf Steiner himself worked with great intensity in various scientific fields to introduce new methods and a new orientation of mind, and something of his intentions is already established. It is not the aim of a Waldorf School to teach the children the philosophy of Steiner or of anyone else: but it is definitely their aim to give their pupils the greatest freedom of mind by acquainting them with all that the modern world has to offer. In spite of the frequent disclaimers of leading scientists (which are indeed not always supported by their utterances when off their guard) that scientific theory is only the best hypothesis yet available, many of the theoretical assumptions of science no less than its practical applications are commonly accepted and taught as fact.

A Waldorf School endeavours to avoid this error by its more historical approach to science. The opening gambit is not the familiar 'Science tells us' but 'This scientist working on these assumptions and under these conditions endeavoured at this time to explain these phenomena by this hypothesis.' It neither sounds, nor is, so simple, but it is the best way in the long run. It is therefore only logical that, before they leave, the children should become familiar with some of the scientific ideas of Rudolf Steiner and their basis, as a part of contemporary life. As it is so much in the public eye today the subject of Physics may perhaps be taken first to illustrate the twofold aim of a Waldorf School in science.

In the ninth and tenth classes the teaching of physics keeps chiefly within the tangible world of everyday experience. The heat engine uses the familiar element of water no less than the old water-wheel. Perhaps it is because it has a certain elemental life that the old steam-engine has still such a fascination for boys. Compared with the internal combustion or electric engine it is a thing of life: it breathes and snorts and perspires and talks a kind of rhythmic speech. Telephone and telegraph also need wires that sing in the wind, or cables that lie full fathom five at the bottom of the sea. In all this we still feel related to the world of the senses. But in the eleventh Grade the modern developments of electricity are studied. The children should know the part that this mysterious, invisible sub-earthly force has played in developing modern views of the nature of substance, in which all its supposed and accepted attributes finally disappear. With this should go the study of the 'machines without moving parts'—radar, radio, television—as characteristic of the twentieth century as were the telescope and microscope of the seventeenth.

Electricity is closely related to modern scientific theories of light. It was at the end of the nineteenth century that Maxwell showed that disturbances in the ether set up by electric and magnetic charges produced waves which travelled at the same speed as light, and hence concluded that light *is* the passage of electric and magnetic forces through the ether. The ether has now disappeared and the waves have become waves of mathematical probability. But the first step in the process began when Newton produced his mechanical theory of light and colour, which left the eye, or the brain, the task of creating the experience of colour out of those ether waves or corpuscles (Newton hovered between the two theories) which the given object emitted. It was not long before facts were found for which Newton's theory could not account, such as the double refraction of Iceland spar. But Newton's fundamental search for a mechanical basis for light and colour was accepted and followed by subsequent scientists.

There was one exception—the German poet Goethe (little as the fact is known) devoted as much time and energy to scientific experimental research as he did to poetry and literature. The important thing about his work is that he did not accept the prevailing point of view that ultimate reality must be conceived in terms of what can be numbered, measured or weighed. This is all the more remarkable because in his day the mechanical material representation of reality was unchallenged and triumphant. No psychologists had postulated an unconscious located nowhere in the human being: no mathematical physicist had conjured away all the sense-pictures of outer substance, shattered the Newtonian conceptions of space and time, and half replaced the old solid world into the mind of the observer. Long before this Goethe denied that the world of number, measure and weight was the ultimate reality. He did not accept Locke's theory that what the senses tell us of the mathematical relations of objects are their primary qualities, while all else are secondary. For him the colour of a rose was as real as all its mathematical relations. He accepted visible colours as what he called 'ultimate phenomena' and he was interested in discovering the laws of their behaviour. Under what natural conditions do colours appear? How does one colour affect another? Are there any primary colours? How and why does the eye create colours as well as receive them? These are some of the questions he investigated, and his investigations led to valuable results. But more important than his results was the fact that he did not treat the physical world as something outside the human mind and indifferent to it—as the scientist did. Mind and world he regarded as a unity: it can be said both that the eye creates the light and that the light creates the eye: man participates in Nature not only because he is physically part of Nature, but in the process of knowing her as well: through man, equally, Nature knows herself.

It was not in the theory of colour alone that Goethe applied his unique method: he worked fruitfully in the spheres of botany and zoology as well. But there is an exceptionally clear demarcation present in the theory of colour between the mathematical theory which isolates man from the phenomenon, and the Goethean view which seeks for Man in Nature and Nature in Man. It happens also that in this domain Rudolf Steiner himself and some of his followers have carried the Goethean view somewhat further than, in the limitations of his time, Goethe was able to do. Thus when the children are learning the modern theory that what we call light is subjective experience, and light is really an electrical or mathematical phenomenon, they should also hear of another view which regards light as objective reality and even reverses the usual relation by speaking, not of light as derived from electricity, but electricity as 'dead' light. The approach to light from this point of view calls for some artistic discrimination. It is a subject which would require a book in itself. But it is important here to stress the general principle of approaching phenomena not only with a photographic but also with a creative eye.

An example from the realm of living things will show a similarity of approach. In the eleventh Class Botany, which has already dealt with photo-synthesis and the plant's relation to light, advances to the study of the cell. The children are shown that a unicellular organism such as the *Chlamydomonas* is entirely complete in itself. The next stage is that in which a number of cells are united together yet each continues a separate life. Then comes the further stage where differentiation between the cells begins, first into the simple sex cells, then into the more complicated functions connected with different parts of the organism. Thus the single cell has within it the capacity for developing into all other cells of all plant organisms. It is a universe in miniature—a microcosm. With its adaptability goes a tremendous power of survival. There is no reason inherent in it why it should make a further step in evolution. When Nature divides it, the division is made by a power from outside it, and the evolution is from the whole to the part. Each cell sacrifices something of its 'wholeness' in order to form a new creation.

In the cell we also see the fundamental differences between the plant and the animal already expressed. The unicellular animal—like the higher animals—has to destroy in order to live. It also has the maximum power of survival. If evolution were towards the survival of the fittest all animals would progress towards the unicellular condition, or would never have aberrated from that ideal state!

It is from such a point of view that the wonderful complexity of cell structure is approached. The new generation should be able to think morphologically as well as atomistically. Fundamentally modern thinking is caught between the alternatives that 'things' must be *either* sense-perceptible objects existing independently of consciousness *or* only ideas in the mind. It is true that some modern physicists are beginning to attribute objective reality to ideas, but this is only in the sphere of mathematics. For Goethe (and for Rudolf Steiner) it was an evident fact that there is an objective realm of creative form perceptible to the mind. Children who have had an artistic education, and whose pictorial imaginative powers have been preserved and fostered, will be especially able to grasp phenomena morphologically.

The study of the cell is a preparation for such thinking, inasmuch as it is a sphere where the whole comes before the part. But Steiner reserved for the last grade that subject where morphological thinking makes what is perhaps the most immediately striking advance in the interpretation of the given data. This is the sphere of zoology.

For in the twelfth Grade a survey of zoology is made, including the wonderful story of the evolution of animal forms. In the geological records of the higher animals the great mystery is the late arrival of man, although the date at which any supposed ancestor of man appears has been placed progressively earlier and earlier. And when he does appear—in the words of one geologist—'Man comes before us geologically with all the signs of mankind upon him—human teeth, upright walk, large brain.' It is a mystery to the mind which thinks exclusively in terms of the material, and is therefore driven to believe that the more perfect form must have evolved from the less perfect. It is not a mystery to the mind which thinks morphologically and can believe that an ideal form may only gradually realise itself in the physical world. In Steiner's view this is the true interpretation of the 'record of the rocks'. The higher animals are all 'end forms', they have completed a specialised evolution in a limited direction. Man could not therefore have evolved from them or from anything like them. But they could have evolved—and in fact did evolve—from the ideal human form, supposing it to have existed in a non-physical state while the animals had already descended into the material. Such an interpretation does indeed account for all the known facts of evolution: the obstacle to its acceptance lies not in them, but in the limitations of modern thinking. A new education exists to help a new generation to overcome those limitations.

The facts which natural science has discovered are nowhere more wonderful than in the sphere of zoology. But that is not a reason for limiting their interpretation to the prevailing scientific outlook. It is the duty of a sound education, as far as in it lies, to consider all possible interpretations, and especially to be sensitive to those changes of mind and heart whose whispers can be heard on moving winds of thought today.

It is a final seal on the work of the twelfth Grade that Steiner reserved for it a study of the art of architecture. For the ultimate secret of architecture is that it is drawn from the human body. The body is a House and a Temple, and it is the source and fountain of all forms and all proportions. It is a secret known to the Christian religion in especial. To live in the body as in a Temple—this is the ultimate gift with which a Waldorf School would wish to send its children into the world.

INDEX